Chesapeake Women
Their Stories ✦ Their Memories

Don Parks

4880 Lower Valley Road • Atglen, PA 19310

Other Schiffer Books by the Author:
Chesapeake Men: Their Stories ~ Their Memories
978-0-7643-4461-9, $24.99

Other Schiffer Books on Related Subjects:
Courageous Women of Maryland
978-0-7643-3541-9, $19.99

17 Women Who Shook the World
978-0-7643-4141-0, $19.99

Designed by Molly Shields
Cover designed by John Cheek
Type set in CaslonOldFace BT/NewBskvll BT

ISBN: 978-0-7643-4701-6
Printed in China

Published by Schiffer Publishing, Ltd.
4880 Lower Valley Road
Atglen, PA 19310
Phone: (610) 593-1777; Fax: (610) 593-2002
E-mail: Info@schifferbooks.com

For our complete selection of fine books on this and related
subjects, please visit our website at www.schifferbooks.com.
You may also write for a free catalog.

This book may be purchased from the publisher. Please
try your bookstore first.

We are always looking for people to write books on new
and related subjects. If you have an idea for a book, please
contact us at proposals@schifferbooks.com.

Schiffer Publishing's titles are available at special discounts
for bulk purchases for sales promotions or premiums.
Special editions, including personalized covers, corporate
imprints, and excerpts can be created in large quantities for
special needs. For more information, contact the publisher.

For Jodi and Morgan...

Devoted Chesapeake women

Acknowledgments

My sincere appreciation is extended to Eddie Somers and Ed Theiler who suggested the idea for a book devoted to women of the Chesapeake. Appreciation is also offered to the women whose stories make up this book. These ladies graciously guided me through the excitement and pitfalls of their lives. For their trust, confidence and willingness to be a part of this project, I am most grateful.

Most of the women who appear on subsequent pages were known to me; however, a few were not. Gratitude is extended to the folks who suggested these women for inclusion in this compendium. These people include Jan and Pam White for suggesting Jeanie Wilson. Eddie Somers for suggesting Shelly Somers. For suggesting Mary Ada Marshall, thanks are extended to Dwight Marshall, and for suggesting Captain Linda Morgan my appreciation is extended to Jean McCommons. Also, my thanks to Annie McLhinney-Cochran for her magnificent photos in Captain Linda Morgan's chapter.

Recognition and thanks are offered to my wife, Linda, for her patience and support during the many hours of research and text preparation. Finally, much appreciation to Mary Sue Traynelis for her editing efforts.

Contents

Introduction

Framed by the Susquehanna River in the north and the mighty Potomac River in the south, Maryland's portion of the Chesapeake Bay continues to delight dreamers, poets, musicians, scientists, and everyone in between. Her mystique and beauty are legendary, as is her sometimes violent nature and unpredictability.

In addition to incubating a large portion of the world's seafood, the Bay has strongly influenced a unique culture and heritage among the people who live along her shores. Few geographical locations have had a more profound effect on their inhabitants than the Chesapeake.

Through the years, Chesapeake citizens have depended on the Bay as a system of transportation. Often, getting from here to there was a lot easier in a boat than traveling the unknown dangers of the overland route. The Bay also provided a livelihood for many who lived beside her pristine waters. The bountiful seafood industry that evolved well into the twentieth century made poor men rich and, sometimes, rich men poor. Ancillary services required by Chesapeake entrepreneurs spurred the economy and added political clout to the region.

Seamen, facing ever-present danger in the Chesapeake, found comfort in a religion that offered hope and a belief that tomorrow would be a better day. Hard work and sacrifice was not unknown to these folks.

Stories of these Chesapeake people abound and the tellers uncountable. They tell of lives fulfilled by interactions with the Bay and her people. Some of their stories are less than happy, but, in the end, most reach a satisfying conclusion.

The eleven women who grace the pages that follow are, as a collection, some of the great Chesapeake storytellers. Their recollections are both informative and entertaining. Without them this book would be meaningless. Some tell of a Bay that was more pristine and wholesome than it is presently and of a time when folks were more humane, not only to their environment, but to each other as well. Hope, nevertheless, remains that their beloved Chesapeake will once again be healthy and the folks who live along her shores will truly be stewards not only of her, but also of each other. We can only hope that their dreams will someday come true.

CHAPTER ONE

Mary Jane Fairbank

Located approximately four miles from the mainland, in the mid-section of Maryland's Eastern Shore, a trio of islands guard the land mass known as Talbot County. Together these islands — Poplar, Jefferson, and Coaches — have a fascinating history.

The largest of the three, Poplar, was originally over 1,500 acres and was known as Popely's Island. It was named by Captain William Claiborne during his exploratory trips to the upper Bay in 1626 and 1627 for an acquaintance, Lieutenant Richard Popely, and was inhabited as early as 1632, becoming the first settlement in Talbot County. Shortly thereafter, land was cleared and a plantation was erected by Claiborne's favorite cousin, Richard Thompson. The Thompson plantation was short-lived, however. In 1637, a tribe of Native Americans raided the island and killed Thompson's family and servants. All of the buildings were burned and the livestock slaughtered. For a time, this ended the settlement of Popely's Island. For the remainder of the century, the island was referred to by a variety of names. Eventually, it was called Poplar, so named for the large number of tulip poplars growing on the island. Poplar Island was occupied in 1813 by British troops during the War of 1812. It is said that the troops supplemented their diets by capturing thousands of crabs that surrounded the island.

In 1847, the island was owned by Charles Carroll, grandson of Charles Carroll of Carrollton, a signer of the Declaration of Independence. The younger Carroll gained information that China was in the market for black cat fur. He decided to turn the island into a fur farm. He advertised that he would pay 25 cents for each female black cat that was brought to him. Along with a few male black cats, he took the females to the island and soon had a burgeoning supply of black cats. He hired a local man to take fish to the island on a daily basis to feed the cats. One especially frigid winter, the Bay froze completely and the waterman was unable to reach the island with the fish. The hungry cats merely walked off the island in search of food, never to be seen again, thus depriving Carroll of his anticipated fortune.

The island went through a succession of owners in the years that followed. Eventually, a town named Valliant appeared on the island. By the late 1800s, Valliant was a town of about a hundred souls and was served by a post office, general store, sawmill, and a school that doubled as a church.

Never as populated as Poplar, Coaches and Jefferson were inhabited by a few settlers who farmed and worked the waters of the Chesapeake to earn a living. By the turn of the twentieth century, the three islands had eroded so badly that only eighty-five hardy settlers remained. By the 1920s, the islands were inhabited only by moonshiners. Revenuers put an end to that endeavor by the end of the decade.

In the later 1920s, high-ranking Democrats became interested in Poplar and Jefferson Islands for use as a retreat and purchased both islands. Maryland Governor Albert Ritchie convinced the Maryland General Assembly to rename both islands "Jefferson," because Democrats upheld the principles of Thomas Jefferson. Coaches was not included in the purchase.

In a short time, a large clubhouse that slept twenty-three was erected on the island that had originally been called Jefferson. There was a suite for the President's use. An eagle was carved in the headboard of the bed. A skeet-shooting range and caretaker's house were built. Duck blinds and a 555-foot pier (the same length as the height of

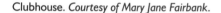

Clubhouse. *Courtesy of Mary Jane Fairbank.*

the Washington Monument) were erécted. A gun room, where members kept hunting and fishing equipment, and an outdoor grill rounded out the amenities. At the time, Jefferson was comprised of thirty-four acres. The adjacent island, once known as Poplar, consisted of 134 acres.

Few clubs can boast of a more dignified membership. Membership in the Jefferson Islands Club was by invitation only and limited to high-ranking democrats. Among the members were United States senators and congressmen, top-level business executives, and prominent leaders of the party. Two Presidents — Franklin Delano Roosevelt and Harry S. Truman — were also active members. It was in this setting that Mary Jane Fairbank lived from 1936 to 1946.

"My father, Varnon (Bunzy) Haddaway, was hired shortly after the island was purchased by the Democrats in 1927," Mary Jane said. "He traveled to the island daily from our home on the mainland. He mostly ran the boats back and forth."

The club owned three boats. Two were typical Chesapeake Bay deadrise designs, about forty feet in length. "They were named *Hound Dog* and *Scotty*," Mary Jane continued. "*Scotty* was named after the President's (FDR) dog Fallah. The boat had a torpedo or drake tail stern. The third boat was a 65-foot yacht named *Jefferson Island*, which ferried many dignitaries from Annapolis. The boat had been donated to the club by a member. Usually, *Hound Dog* and *Scotty* traveled back and forth from nearby Lowe's Wharf to the island."

Varnon got his nickname while growing up in Tilghman. His mother had died when he was 11 and he worked in a bakery before and after school each day. In the morning, the bakery owners would give him a bun or two and he'd stuff them into his hip pockets as he walked to school. "The kids would see him and yell, 'Here comes old Buns,'" said Mary Jane. "Through the years, Buns was altered to Bunzy. A lot of people didn't know his real name, all they knew was Bunzy. After he married, my mother was called Mrs. Bunzy and my brother, Little Bunzy."

Aerial view of Jefferson Island. *Courtesy of Mary Jane Fairbank.*

Hobson and Nora Jones were caretakers living in a house among the buildings of the Jefferson Islands Club. They cooked and looked after guests when they came. "Daddy came home one night in 1936 and told my mother (Alice) that they needed somebody to take Miss Nora's and Mr. Hobson's places on the island," Mary Jane explained. "The couple was planning to retire. By that time daddy had been appointed manager and he asked if mother was interested in taking over Miss Nora's duties. Mother agreed to take the job and off we went to Jefferson Island. It was a place where I would spend some of the happiest years of my life."

The Haddaways would, ultimately, become quite popular among the politicians who visited the island. They were well liked and considered "family" by many of the club members. Bunzy had a special relationship with guests who visited the island.

"Tallulah Bankhead was the daughter of Speaker of the House, William Bankhead," the affable Mary Jane explained. "She was a Hollywood actress who was very controversial. Very flamboyant, she dressed in silk blouses and wore lots of jewelry. She referred to everyone as 'dahling.' She told it like it was, no holds were barred. She was Hollywood through and through. Tallulah visited the island a couple of times with her dad while I was there. One day she asked my father to take her over to the big island (Poplar) to go fox hunting. Dad took her over there and she saw a fox and yelled, 'Talley Ho.' Dad got a big kick out of that and from then on he'd call her 'Talley Ho.' When he'd call her that, she'd just look at him and moan, 'Oh, Captain.'

"Tallulah had a good friend who was a devout Catholic. Through her, she had become friends with a priest. She was attending a wedding one time that her friend, the priest, was officiating. Following the ceremony, the priest was walking down the center aisle waving a container of incense. When he saw Tallulah, he stopped and said, 'Tallulah, it's good to see you. You look lovely, I love your dress.' Tallulah looked at him and replied, 'I love your dress too, father, but it's on fire.' The incense burner had set his robe ablaze."

When Tallulah died, she was buried near Chestertown, at a church named St. Paul's. "I visited her grave one time and on her tombstone was a pair of sunglasses and silk flowers," Mary Jane said.

Mary Jane and her family lived in a cottage not far from the lodge where the politicians gathered. "Our house had four bedrooms, a bathroom, and a sitting room," she stated. "We ate all our meals over at the club house. Besides my parents, there were two other men who worked there. One of the men was a butler named Rufus.

"Rufus had been on the island for a long time. He'd worked there even before my dad went there. He was definitely a part of our family. He had no family of his own. He lived in a couple of rooms in the cabin that held the gun room. He

Haddaway family. *Courtesy of Mary Jane Fairbank.*

was very protective of my brother and me. He'd take me in a rowboat to a spot where there was a real clear smooth bottom. That's where I learned to swim.

"At Christmastime, he'd select our presents from the Sears catalog and send for them. On Christmas morning, it didn't matter how early we got up, Rufus would be sitting in a chair in our sitting room waiting for us to come downstairs. He'd be holding his gifts for us in his lap. He really practically raised me."

Following the move to the island, Mary Jane and her brother, Eugene (Little Bunzy), traveled to the mainland each day to attend school. "I was only five when we moved there," she recalled. "My brother was two years older. I was in first grade. We'd get up way before daybreak and daddy would take us over to Lowe's Wharf in one of the boats. It was a half-hour boat ride; we'd get off the boat and walk a mile to the main road and wait for the school bus to pick us up for the ride to Tilghman Island (joined to the mainland by bridge) and the elementary school there. I went to Tilghman Elementary for four years.

"In winter, when the Bay froze over, we'd stay on the mainland with our grandparents in McDaniel until the thaw came. When we lived in McDaniel, our Principal, Raymond Jump, would pick us up on his way by our house and take us to Tilghman. He lived in St. Michaels and would give us a ride as he was on his way to school. Later, our grandparents moved to Claiborne and we went to the schools in St. Michaels.

"I just loved living on Jefferson Island. There were different people visiting all the time. It was really busy on weekends, especially in summer. In the winter, it was mostly men and they came to hunt, but in the summer lots of families came over. They'd bring kids with them and I'd make friends and we'd play together. As a youngster, I didn't realize the importance of the guests that visited.

"Senator Hawes of Missouri visited the island frequently. One time he stayed for six weeks. He always stayed in the President's Suite. He brought his family to the island once. He had a daughter named Peyton and we became good friends. While the Senator was away on business, Mrs. Hawes sent for me and I spent a week in Washington. That was my first trip there. I was about eleven at the time. Their chauffer, Alfonso, drove us around the city and showed us all the sights. One of the places he took me was inside the statue that sits on top of the Capitol. This was closed to the public, but Alfonso lifted me up so that I could see out of the eyes of the statue and look all over the city. I had a marvelous time; we even had lunch in the Senate Dining Room.

"I had a Chesapeake Bay Retriever who was my best friend on the island. Her name was Duchess and everywhere I went, she was by my side. My mother wouldn't allow Duchess to sleep in the bed with me, though. Every night Duchess would lie beside my bed on a rug until mom went to bed and then she'd hop up onto my bed and sleep with me. In the morning, as soon as she heard commotion in the house, she'd jump off the bed and get back on her rug.

"I also had a great big yellow angora cat. The cat and dog were the best of friends. The cat would sleep on the dog's back whenever it had a chance. One day we had a hard storm while the cat was out on the pier. The wind from the storm picked up the cat and threw it into the water. Duchess saw what happened and ran out on the pier, jumped into the water, and grabbed the cat by the scruff of the neck and swam to shore with her. The cat was okay after that.

"I was never lonely living on the island. Besides all the visitors, I'd have my mainland friends over and they'd spend a few days with me. There was always a lot going on, especially in the summer."

Among the thirty-five charter members of the club were President Franklin Delano Roosevelt, Vice President John Nance Gardner, and Postmaster General James Farley.

14

Mary Jane, her mother, and Duchess. *Courtesy of Mary Jane Fairbank.*

The congressmen included representatives William Bankhead of Alabama and Parker Corning from New York, while the senators were Millard Tydings of Maryland, Peter Gerry of Rhode Island, Royal Copeland of New York, Harry B. Hawes of Missouri, Key Pittman of Nevada, Joseph Robinson of Arkansas, Robert Wagner from New York, and David Welch from Massachusetts. Additionally, there were numerous CEOs of major companies, such as August Busch of Anheuser-Busch, Inc. and Tom Watson, President of IBM. The President of General Electric was also a member.

As the club gained inertia, the number of members drastically increased. "When Harry S. Truman assumed the Presidency, he refused to pay the $500 annual membership fee, plus the cost of meals," Mary Jane laughed. "Club officials allowed him to be an honorary member.

"Those men really had some wild parties on the island. I remember one time when Senator Pittman had a bit too much to drink. He was in the lodge, sitting on a couch facing the fireplace, and he pulled out two pearl-handled revolvers and shot out both carriage lights over the fireplace.

"Senator Pittman got bored one day and asked my dad to take him across the Bay to Solomons in the club boat. Dad took him over there; it was a very long trip. Dad dropped the Senator off in Solomons and headed back home. When he got back to Jefferson Island, many hours later, and walked into the lodge, Senator Pittman was sitting there grinning at him.

"One year the Senator and his wife came to the island for Christmas. On Christmas morning, he watched our family open their presents. He apparently had never before witnessed anything like that; the couple had no children of their own. The next day, he went to the bank and got lots of quarters and roamed around the mainland, handing them out to migrant workers."

Guests ate family-style in the dining room of the lodge. "A senator from Kentucky had been drinking entirely too much," Mary Jane explained. "While he was eating

Clubhouse porch. *Courtesy of Mary Jane Fairbank.*

FDR seated at table. *Courtesy of Mary Jane Fairbank.*

dinner, he passed out and his face ended up in a bowl of mashed potatoes. My dad cleaned him up and moved him away from the table so he could sleep it off.

"In 1945, a businessman named Russell Arundel and an executive from the Pepsi-Cola company threw a 'bash' on the island. It was shortly after VJ Day and over a thousand people came to the party. President Truman was to be in attendance and the Secret Service was everywhere. The Navy and Coast Guard, with guns at ready, constantly patrolled the waters around the island. It was exciting!

"In addition to politicians, war heroes and businessmen were in attendance. Alcohol was brought in by the case. Sixty cases of scotch alone were brought over. Every kind of drink imaginable was served that day. Bartenders were imported from the mainland and there was additional help in the kitchen. Boats were busy all day ferrying guests back and forth to the island.

"President Truman arrived and he wanted to eat his dinner out on the porch. We moved everything out there to obey his wishes and set up for the evening meal. I was waiting tables. I was fourteen at the time. Guests ate family-style. I had a dish of peas in each hand and when I went to place a bowl in front of the President the other dish tilted and peas spilled down his back. I was embarrassed and didn't know what to say

Mary Jane Fairbank seated at FDR table. *Photo by author.*

or do. President Truman just looked at me and said, 'Oh hell honey, don't worry about that. You'll have something to tell your grandchildren.'

"The President requested that a piano be available during his visit and one was brought over and placed on the porch. President Truman played the piano and Morton Downey, a popular Irish tenor at the time, lifted me up and plopped me on top of the piano. The President asked me what I wanted to sing. I asked if he knew 'Mexicali Rose.' He played and Morton Downey and I sang that song and all the show tunes of the day.

"Truman was a real character. He could cuss like the best of them. He had a fowl mouth, but he was approachable and down to earth. He was a very interesting man."

The next day, Truman harbored a desire to go fishing and planned a trip for early the following morning. He invited several of the guests to go with him, but they all refused. In desperation, he had Bunzy take only himself. "He caught lots of fish and when he and my dad returned to the club he had dad ring the bell that was on the lawn in a vigorous manner," Mary Jane smiled. "Thinking there was an emergency, people came out on the lawn in a hurry. As the bell continued to ring, people were running out of the lodge, some still putting on their clothes. After they were all out on the lawn, the President stood there with the fish he'd caught and announced, 'I just wanted you SOBs to see what you missed.'

"After the 'bash,' there was lots of food left over. There were gallons of maraschino cherries left on the island. I decided I'd make myself a milkshake using some of the cherries. After I drank my milkshake, I got deathly sick. I've never been able to eat a maraschino cherry since."

Mary Jane's grandmother's sister had a good friend, Mrs. Byers, who lived on the mainland. She was wealthy and getting along in years. Eventually, her health became an issue and necessitated placement in a nursing facility. "She had a cat that she named David," Mary Jane said. "She was very protective of that cat and was worried to death about what would happen to it when she went into the nursing home. My grandmother's sister told her she thought she knew the perfect place for the cat. She explained about our family living on the island, where there were no cars or traffic to interfere with David's wellbeing. Mrs. Byers was impressed, but I still had to go over there, meet with her, and have an interview before she would allow David to travel to the island with me. The interview went well and David and I headed for home. I held David in my arms all the way back to Jefferson Island. As we reached the island, I put David up on the pier in order to climb out of the boat. That cat ran off the pier and took off. I've never seen it since. I looked all over the island, but no David. For days, I roamed around searching for him. I put out food, but David was nowhere to be found. Later, Mrs. Byers would ask grandmother's friend how David was adjusting over on the island. She'd answer that he was fine; he just loved roaming about that island."

When the Democrats purchased the islands, there was another family living there. "A man and woman lived in a house on the island," Mary Jane explained. "They had two children, a boy and a girl. The boy was my age and the girl was the same age as my brother. We all played together from time to time. When the children became school-aged, their father refused to send them to school. He said that he'd teach them all he knew and that was all they needed to know. The authorities pressured him to send them to school, but he still refused. Finally, club members told him that if he didn't send them to school he'd have to move off the island.

"Still refusing, he moved his family to neighboring Coaches Island. There was a vacant house over there where wild goats lived. The man cleaned up the house, moved out the goats, and moved his family in. He never did send his children to school.

"The old man had a tremendous garden and he'd bring us vegetables throughout the summer. When he came, his daughter would often tag along with him. She had a crush on my brother. One time, as the family was walking down the dock heading for their boat for the return trip to Coaches, his daughter was carrying a basket and turned to my brother and said, 'I'd like to put you right in this basket and take you home with me.'"

Jefferson was separated from Poplar by a very narrow channel. "It was really no more than a mud flat," said Mary Jane. "There was only about six or eight feet between the northern tip of Jefferson and the northern tip of Poplar.

"Mrs. Walker McKay Jones was a frequent visitor to the island. She and her husband lived on a big horse farm in Middlebury, Virginia. When she came, she brought her secretary, Mercedes Marcado.

"Mrs. Jones loved to fish. She'd rather fish than eat when she was starving. Every time she came, she'd charter a boat out of Tilghman to take her fishing. The owner of the boat was Milton Cummings. When the fishing trip was finished, she'd ask Capt. Cummings if there were any peelers (used for bait) left over. There would usually be a few left over and Cummings would give them to her.

"That evening, either my brother or I would row her through the narrow channel between the islands and she'd fish until all the peelers were gone. One night it was high tide when we went through the narrow channel. After Mrs. Jones used up all her bait, we headed back to Jefferson Island. The tide had dropped by then and we couldn't get through. We had to row all the way around Jefferson Island to get back to the pier. That was quite a chore. Later, she brought me the first rod and reel that I ever owned."

One of the members of the club was an army general named Gilmore. He and his wife were fond of Mary Jane and brought her a present. "It was a doll," smiled Mary Jane. "I still have that doll and I treasure it."

Walter Edmonson was an executive of the Schwinn Bicycle Company and a frequent visitor to the island. "One day he decided to have a barbeque," Mary Jane laughed. "He prepared a barbeque pit and went over to Coaches Island and brought back one of the wild goats. All day long he cooked that goat. Mom made a sauce to baste the goat and he worked hard, turning and basting the goat. After eating, my very Victorian grandmother, who was visiting, asked, 'Mr. Edmonson, how was the goat?' 'My God, grandma!' he replied. 'That was the toughest thing I've ever tried to eat. And just think that I spent all day long mopping that goat's ass.' My straight-laced grandmother almost died when he said that. Mr. Edmonson always promised to bring me a bicycle, but he never did."

James Forrestal was the Secretary of the Navy during the Roosevelt years and a frequent visitor to the island. Mary Jane spoke with him and looked forward to his visits. "I thought he was a nice man," she recalled fondly. "We talked for a long time and we really hit it off. I didn't realize who the man was at the time. I just thought he was very pleasant.

"Years later, someone told me that Forrestal was really difficult to get along with. I didn't find him that way at all. It was almost like we were talking about two different people. Ironically, my grandson, who is a Lieutenant Commander in the Navy, recently flew from the aircraft carrier, *USS Forrestal*."

In March of 1946, a devastating fire erupted in the Presidential Suite of the lodge. The fire was due to faulty wiring. The clubhouse was completely destroyed, thus putting an end to the Jefferson Islands Club. The island was sold shortly thereafter.

"Living on the island taught me some valuable life lessons," said Mary Jane. "We lived an isolated existence — there were no telephones or televisions and there was no communication with the outside world. When I left the island to go to school, for example, I had to be very organized and planned in order to prepare for the day. There was no library and I couldn't call a friend to get assignments. I think my organizational skills today stem from my life on the island."

After the fire, Mary Jane's family moved to the mainland. Her parents had previously purchased a home in a nearby town. "We lost a lot of our personal belongings in the fire," she regretfully explained. "There were sets of china that had belonged to my parents and many other items that were used in the club kitchen. All were lost!"

Club members purchased another island in the Potomac River named St. Catherine's following the fire on Jefferson. In time, the Chesapeake swallowed up that island and the club ceased to exist.

In 1948, Jefferson and Poplar Islands were purchased by George Bailey. The Baileys built a lodge on the site of the original clubhouse. Their lodge was known as Poplar Islands Lodge. The ramp that was built for FDR's wheelchair was retained and abutted up to the porch. The spacious lodge contained several bedrooms and offered fine amenities.

Bunzy was hired by the Baileys to once again bring guests to the island and lead hunting and fishing parties. "The islands were a popular spot for nesting crows and my father guided many hunting trips," said Mary Jane. "Crow hunts took place at night. Many times daddy would make several trips a night, bringing hunters back and forth to the island. In addition to hunting and fishing, he also took the Bailey children to and from school on a daily basis.

"In 1951, when I got married, the Baileys gave my husband and me a set of dishes as a wedding present. I've always treasured those dishes. I still have them. Mr. Bailey died in the early 1950s and the island was again sold. This ended my family's involvement with Jefferson Island."

It was fifty years before Mary Jane neared the shoreline of Jefferson Island again. "My son took me over there in his boat. We didn't go ashore, but we were very close to the island," she said remorsefully. "I could see that a lot of the island had washed away. After Poplar Island started to erode and Jefferson lost its protection, the north winds eroded much of Jefferson. Now it's about a third the size it was when I lived there.

"I've always said that I'd move back to the island tomorrow if I had the chance, but, after seeing the extent that the island eroded, I don't know that I could do that. It made me sick just to see how much of it was gone.

"I've never set foot on the island since our family left there. I'd love to go back and roam around a bit. I'd like to go back and visit the cottage where we lived. The cottage suffered no harm from the fire. I'd like to see my old bedroom and that sort of thing."

Intelligent, articulate, insightful, and witty, Mary Jane Fairbank's years of living on Jefferson Island are remembered with fondness. "I had a wonderful childhood," she said. "I loved Jefferson Island and wouldn't trade the memories of living there for anything."

CHAPTER TWO

Shelly Somers

"My husband says he was a city boy from Ewell who married a country girl from Rhodes Point," laughed Shelly Somers, as she described her courtship and eventual marriage to Eddie Somers. "In those days, the 'city' where he lived had a population of approximately 250."

Ewell and Rhodes Point are communities on Smith Island, Maryland's sole offshore inhabited island. Actually an archipelago, the island is composed of three islets. The largest of these is uninhabited by humans and home to the Martin National Wildlife Preserve. A neighboring islet is home to the villages of Ewell and Rhodes Point. Tylerton, the third Smith Island community, is located on the third islet.

Accessible from the other two only by boat, Tylerton, with a full-time population of fifty-one, is the farthest south of the three communities. To reach Tylerton from the other villages requires a two-mile boat ride. The islet on which it is located nears the Maryland/Virginia boundary and is surrounded by the waters of Tangier Sound. With a population of forty-five, Rhodes Point is the westernmost Smith Island community and is closest to the broad expanse of the Chesapeake Bay. Of the three communities, Ewell is the most insular and, therefore, the most protected from the sometimes harsh Chesapeake weather. Today, Ewell, the "city" where Eddie Somers grew up, has a full-time population of 125. The villages of Tylerton and Ewell have their own post offices while residents of Rhodes Point are served by the post office in Ewell.

Named for an early landowner, Henry Smith, the island sits roughly in the center of the southern portion of Maryland's Chesapeake Bay. Located twelve miles from Maryland's Eastern Shore mainland and fourteen miles from the Western Shore mainland, the island measures approximately eight by four miles. Barely above sea level, Smith Island is surrounded by valuable salt marshes that provide habitat for a variety of Chesapeake animals and plants.

Born in her grandparents' home in Rhodes Point, Shelly Somers' formative years were spent on the island. "My parents, Lester and Nancy Tyler, were living with my grandmother when I made my initial appearance into the world," she said. "They were in the process of building their own home and were living with my grandparents at the time. My mother wanted to remain on Smith Island for the delivery." In those days, a doctor lived on the island. Shelly's Aunt Gloria assisted the doctor with the delivery.

A brother, Lechy, was two years older than Shelly. Shelly's parents, with the help of her father's brother, finished the home where the family would eventually live in the early 1960s. "My brother sat on the steps and cried his eyes out," Shelly laughed. "He cried for two or three nights. He wanted to go back home where his grandmother lived, about one hundred feet away from our new house." A second brother, Brad, would come along fifteen years after Shelly's birth. "Mom and dad were older when he was born," she said. "I was really like a second mother to my younger brother; I helped raise him."

Shelly's grandfather had died when her dad was a teenager. During the winter season, when she got older, Shelly's grandmother lived with a daughter in Crisfield. In the summer, she returned to Smith Island.

Shelly's great-grandmother was originally from Warrenton, Virginia. She had lived on a plantation there. Her cousin lived on Smith Island and she would come to the island for visits. She met her husband, an island native, married, and relocated to Rhodes Point.

Ewell Post Office. *Photo by author.*

"My grandmother's sister, Otilia, grew up on Smith Island," said Shelly. "She left the island in order to attend high school back in Virginia. In Virginia, she lived with her grandparents." Returning to Smith Island after graduation, she attended nursing school at the McCready Hospital in Crisfield. In the 1930s, she traveled to Arizona to work on Indian Reservations. Following her stint in Arizona, she came back to Maryland and, later in life, married the postmaster in Crisfield.

Like many residents on the southern portion of Maryland's Eastern Shore, Shelly's ancestors had migrated to this country from Wales. Many of the men from Wales had earned a living as fishermen and brought considerable seafaring skills with them. These skills would ultimately be used as they worked the waters of the Chesapeake Bay.

Always industrious, Shelly learned entrepreneurship at an early age. "When I was nine or ten years old, I'd go around the community cutting grass," she explained. "The Rhodes Point Methodist Church would ask for bids to cut the grass surrounding the church each year. As a teenager, I'd always submit a bid and usually got the job. Because I was young, I suppose my bid was always lower than any of the older people."

During the warmth of summer, many crabbers on Smith Island used crab scrapes as a method for catching crabs. In Maryland, scraping is allowed only in the county of Somerset, where Smith Island is located. Crab scraping involves the use of six-foot triangular iron frames with a four-foot width. Attached to the after end of the frame is a net bag with a two-inch mesh extending about eight feet. Similar to the oyster dredge but without the teeth that dig into the Chesapeake's bottom, scrapes are pulled through the underwater grasses abundant in that part of the Bay. As the scrape travels over the bottom, crabs that are in the area are forced into the mesh bag by the boat's momentum and captured. Pulling the scrape aboard by hand, the waterman extricates the crabs from the bag and returns the scrape to the water for the next "lick" or pass. The goal of the crab scraper is to catch peelers and soft crabs. These are more valuable than the more plentiful hard crabs.

Crab scraping boats. *Photo by author.*

Specially-designed workboats are used for crab scraping. About thirty feet in length, these open boats are very low sided in order to ease the burden of lifting the heavy scrapes aboard. Crab scraping is laborious and strenuous work.

"Sometimes my dad would catch diamondback terrapin (turtles) in his scrapes," said Shelly. "There were two men on Rhodes Point that would buy terrapin. Each day I would check with my dad when he came ashore to see if he had caught any terrapin. Usually there might be one or two caught. I'd go aboard his boat and round up the terrapin. If there was more than one, I'd put them in a basket and walk across the bridge to the men who would buy them. I'd find out how much each of them was paying that day and deliver my terrapin to the man who paid the most.

"If I only had one terrapin, I'd put one hand under his bottom shell and the other over the top shell. That way the terrapin couldn't scratch me with its claws. I'd also sometimes take one of my doll blankets and wrap the turtle in it, again to protect myself from its claws. If the turtle was wrapped in a blanket, I'd carry it like a baby.

"One day, as I was carrying a turtle heading toward the buyer, I saw something on the road and bent down to pick it up. When I did, the terrapin bit me on the chin. I was standing on the bridge screaming for help. Dad rushed toward me as I stood there with the terrapin hanging from my chin. I learned not to bend over with a turtle in my hand after that experience."

Shelly in restaurant uniform. *Courtesy of Shelly Somers.*

Shelly's mother would often take Shelly with her when she went netting for crabs. Netting is accomplished by standing on the bow (front) of the boat with a crab net at the ready. Looking down into the submerged aquatic vegetation (sav), when a crab was spotted the crabber would deftly scoop it off the bottom. "I was very young when mom took me with her," Shelly said. "She would have me sit in the boat real still-like. I didn't like that; it was too confining. I wanted to be roaming around the shore to see what I might find."

During her middle school years, Shelly earned enough money to buy all her own clothing. "I liked making my own money," she said. "I enjoyed buying necessities and helping out the family."

Among the better Smith Island crab scrapers, Shelly's dad actively worked his scrapes until three years ago. "He was eighty years old when he finally stopped scraping," Shelly explained. "He was devoted to crabbing. All the younger watermen would finish their work and come in for the day, but daddy would still be out there working. He loved it! I tried to get him to stop crabbing, but he wouldn't. My husband, Eddie, told me to stop worrying about him. 'Stop worrying so much about him,' he said. 'He's happy out there. He's doing exactly what he wants to be doing.'"

In addition to her other entrepreneurial pursuits, Shelly began working in a local restaurant when she was thirteen. The restaurant, the only one in the community, was called The Bayside Inn. Tour boats from the mainland would dock at the restaurant and come in for a meal. "I would wait tables at the restaurant until the tour boats stopped coming," she stated, "and then I'd go and mow my lawns."

Many Smith Islanders maintain shanties on the waterfront, where Bay water is pumped into large tanks containing peeler crabs. In their final stages, peelers are crabs that are about to shed their shell (molt) and become soft crabs. Someone is charged with monitoring the tanks and extracting the crabs as they finish the shedding process and become soft. Soft crabs have always held more value than hard crabs. Placed in wooden trays surrounded by sea grass, soft crabs are later taken to the mainland for processing.

"One year, when I was about sixteen, daddy's shantyman quit," Shelly said. "I told daddy I thought I could tend to the shanty. He agreed to let me try. I'd get up very early and fish up the crabs at the shanty, pack them up for shipment, and put them in a skiff; then I'd paddle over to the bridge where a truck picked them up and took them to the dock in Ewell for shipment to Crisfield. All of this had to be accomplished before 7 a.m. After that, I'd mow my lawns and work in the restaurant. I was a shantywoman for several years before entering college."

Like many islanders, in the warmer months, Shelly seldom wore shoes. A jug of gasoline was stationed on the back steps of her home for the purpose of cleaning road tar from her feet before entering the house.

One day, as she was riding her bicycle over the bridge, she saw a snake sunning itself on the bridge deck. She decided to run over the snake. As she did, the snake reared up and bit her on the ankle. "I wouldn't have been bitten if I'd had shoes on," Shelly explained. The snake was not poisonous.

"Rhodes Point was a lot different in those days than it is now," Shelly said. "I remember when there were three grocery stores in the community. There were over one hundred people living there then."

Crab shanty. *Photo by author.*

Shelly's father and four other family members owned a dredge boat named *Minnie V*, a skipjack. Indigenous to the Chesapeake Bay, skipjacks evolved during the oyster boom of the latter half of the nineteenth century. During the boom times of the oyster fishery, boats from New York and beyond invaded Maryland's oyster beds. Schooners and steam-powered vessels came to the Bay in search of the bivalve. Fearing the oyster population might be depleted as it had been in Long Island Sound, in 1865 state lawmakers closed the Chesapeake to dredging by outsiders and imposed strict sanctions on Marylanders who wished to continue the process. Only native Marylanders were allowed to dredge for oysters and dredging had to be done by means of sail power only. Steam-powered vessels could no longer be utilized for oyster dredging in state waters.

With a very large mainsail and small jib, skipjacks drag iron triangular dredges over the oyster beds. The dredges, about eight feet in width, have teeth on their bottom edge that allow them to dig into the bottom. Oysters are collected in chain bags attached to the trailing edge of the dredge. Propelled over the bottom by the boat's momentum, a heavy oyster-laden dredge might weigh eight hundred pounds or more. To hoist the dredge aboard, a donkey engine is on deck. Prior to the use of engines, crewmembers hoisted dredges aboard with hand-operated winches.

Because Maryland law precludes the use of internal propulsion aboard skipjacks, twelve- to fourteen-foot push boats, or yawl boats, hang on davits from the after end of

Skipjack under sail. *Photo by author*.

the boat. These boats are powered by inboard engines and are used to push the skipjack into and out of port.

The *Minnie V* was built in 1906 in the Somerset County town of Wenona. Measuring forty-five feet on deck and with a beam (width) of sixteen feet, the boat still sails today. With her centerboard retracted, the boat draws three feet of water.

Following her oystering days, the boat was owned by an outdoor educational organization and utilized for ecotours. More recently, the vessel has been based on the Potomac River and takes passengers on excursions from National Harbor.

Before the advent of skipjacks, schooners and sailing vessels called bugeyes were used to dredge for oysters. The deep-drafted schooners disallowed entry into shallower waters where many of the bivalves were located. Generally larger than skipjacks, bugeyes are essentially dugout canoes.

Canoes originated with Native Americans. Early settlers found that larger boats could be constructed by pinning a number of logs together and then hollowing them out. Eventually, up to nine logs were pinned together in this manner. The bugeye was the result.

Typically, bugeyes were fifty feet or more in length. The *John Branford*, however, was eighty-five feet long. Low sided and equipped with a centerboard, bugeyes traditionally had two masts. The mainsail was attached to the after mast. A small jib rounded out the sail plan. Double-ended bugeyes had patent sterns. These sterns were beams placed above the waterline atop the pointed after sections of the vessel, which also provided a location where the push boat davits were fastened.

Expensive to build, in time watermen began investigating alternative vessels for use in oyster dredging. Skipjacks were the result. Skipjacks are of traditional plank on frame construction and much less costly to build than bugeyes. By the turn of the twentieth century, a thousand skipjacks worked the waters of the Chesapeake. Today, Chesapeake Bay skipjacks make up the only remaining commercial sailing fleet in the United States.

"During winters, daddy was always gone on the skipjack," said Shelly. "The *Minnie V* would leave on Sunday afternoons and wouldn't return until the following Friday evening. During the week, the crew would sell the oysters they'd caught to buyboats. They'd live on the skipjack all week. It was a cold and damp existence. While daddy was away on the skipjack, the women would gather in various homes and have card parties and other activities. I remember playing a card game called 'Rook.'"

In spite of the isolation, Shelly's generation found lots of activities to take up spare time. "Over in Tylerton they had a community center," she explained. "Every Saturday we'd go over there and roller skate in the community center. We had our own skates; I even made pompoms for mine. We had a great time."

During the summer, Shelly and her friends spent a great deal of time swimming. "When I was little, I'd wear a life jacket, but when I got big enough that daddy thought I could learn to swim he taught me to swim the Smith Island way," Shelly explained. "He'd tie a line (rope) around my waist and tell me to jump off the boat. If I failed to swim, he'd pull me back to the boat with the line. It's amazing how fast you learn to swim when you have to." Both Shelly and her brother learned to swim in Parks' Canal, where the water was fifteen feet deep. Her father would take them there in his scrape boat.

As Shelly grew older, she and her friends swam from the county wharf. "On Sundays, everybody would go around in their boats," she said. "Boats were like pick-up trucks and cars in other communities. Teenagers would gather at the county wharf and the boys from Tangier (Virginia's only inhabited offshore island) would come over and join us. Sometimes we'd borrow a skiff and go over to the Bay side and lay on the beach. Kids would gather there on weekends.

Bugeye under sail. *Photo by author.*

"We'd also go fishing sometimes. One time I had two flounders on my line at the same time. We didn't have rod and reels; we used twine with hooks attached. Twine would be wound around a cork float. I asked daddy for help getting the fish off the line. He just looked at me and said, 'That's your problem.'"

When she began dating Eddie, the pair spent a great deal of time looking for arrowheads. Once used by Native Americans, arrowheads were made from stone and were an important component of their weaponry. "We'd go around picking them up," Shelly said. "Every weekend was spent looking for arrowheads. Through the years, we've collected between 250 and 300 of them. We still enjoy doing that every chance we get."

Shelly's grandfather was mate on the *J. C. Widener*, a buoy tender owned by the state of Maryland. Still active, the vessel is approximately seventy-five feet long. The *Widener* is charged with maintaining state-owned aids to navigation (buoys) in Maryland's portion of the mid-Bay. The *Widener* also serves as an ice-breaker in times of inclement weather. The vessel has the capability of breaking ice six to eight inches thick.

Several years ago, when the annual skipjack races were held near Annapolis, the *Widener* would travel to Sandy Point State Park near the Chesapeake Bay Bridges. "Grandmother would go up there on the *Widener* and sometimes I'd go along with her,"

Shelly said. "Lots of state dignitaries would come out to the boat as it was anchored off the Park to watch the races. Grandmother would cook for the guests and I would help her. It was exciting being around all those high-ranking state officials and watching the skipjacks race."

During her high school years, Shelly enrolled in an EMT class sponsored by the University of Maryland. Because she wasn't eighteen, she was required to get special permission to attend. "One night, after finishing my EMT training, I was called to a house on the island," said Shelly. "The woman who lived there was pregnant and she was home alone. Her husband was off working on a tugboat. She was having some difficulty with the pregnancy and there was vaginal bleeding. It was extremely cold outside and the island was frozen in. I knew we had to get the woman off the island. We called for a helicopter, but they didn't want to come because of the weather. It was snowing and blowing hard. We pleaded with the paramedic assigned to the state police helicopter. There was nothing we could do for the woman except try to prevent shock. The helicopter finally arrived and took the woman to the hospital in Salisbury. Both she and the baby were okay. The baby did suffer some distress because of blood loss, however."

Graduating from Crisfield High School in 1978, Shelly traveled daily to the mainland to attend high school. "It was a 45-minute boat ride each way to get to school," she said. "Some days it was a rough ride. If it was thick fog outside, we wouldn't have to attend school that day. After getting to Crisfield, a bus would meet us at the dock and take us to the school. Those of us from Smith Island couldn't stay at the school for extra-curricular activities like sports, etc. We couldn't stay after the regular school hours because we had to leave when the school boat left. I would've loved to have played sports."

In 1977, there was a severe freeze in the Bay. "I stayed with a cousin on the mainland for two months so I could attend school," said Shelly. "I only got home by way of helicopter. I was only able to get home twice during those two months."

Since her middle school years, Shelly knew she wanted to be a nurse. Following graduation from high school, she enrolled in the nursing program at Salisbury State University (SSU). She graduated with a bachelor's in nursing in 1982.

In 1981, Shelly's father became ill. Initially admitted to Peninsula General Hospital in Salisbury, he later entered the Marine Hospital in Baltimore. Diagnosed with Multiple Sclerosis because of numbness in his extremities, he was eventually transferred to a rehabilitation hospital in Salisbury. In late spring of 1981, he was released and went home to Rhodes Point.

"Daddy was not feeling well, but he really wanted to go crabbing," Shelly explained. "There was no income coming into the household and things were a little strained. By then, I had finished my junior year at SSU, so I told daddy, 'Okay, let's go crabbing!' We'd go out crab scraping every day. I did most of the heavy work while he culled the crabs after I'd pull in the scrapes. At about noon, I'd say, 'Okay, it's time to stop, we need to go home now.' He'd respond, 'Just one more lick.' Eventually, I'd persuade him to go in. We'd work together getting the crabs in. Later, in the afternoon, I'd go and fish up the crabs in the shanty. Most of the time he wasn't feeling well; I really worked hard that summer."

December of 1980 was memorable. Shelly and Eddie became engaged. "Eddie was three years ahead of me in school," She explained. "We had been seeing each other for some time and, during my sophomore year in college, ours became a serious relationship. In December 1981, before my final semester at the University, we were married. We were married on the 25th wedding anniversary of my parents.

"Eddie's and my mother started planning for our wedding the summer before. They made all the food for the wedding. They took charge. We had a large wedding; ten people stood up with us."

After their marriage, the young couple relocated to Crisfield. In order to find employment, Shelly understood there would be a need to move from the island.

"A tradition in our family is that each Christmas everyone gathers at the home of my parents," said Shelly. "The first Christmas Eddie and I were married, we went back to Rhodes Point. We shared in another family tradition of having homemade scrapple and coconut Smith Island cake. After we arrived on the island, the Bay started to freeze up. I was supposed to work the following day; it was frustrating. I was working at the McCready Hospital in Crisfield and I was afraid I wouldn't be able to get back to the mainland for work. We were finally able to persuade one of the boat captains to take us back to the mainland and I made it to work on time. That was a stressful situation."

Shelly's nursing career has exceeded twenty years. Currently, she is employed by the Somerset County Department of Health and is looking forward to retirement in a few years.

Now eighty-three, Shelly's father continues to live on Smith Island. Shelly's mother died a couple of years ago.

In 2004, Shelly and Eddie bought the house that was located behind her parents' home. After renovation, they maintained the house for the next two or three years before deciding to sell it. "A lady from Baltimore bought it," said Shelly. "In addition to the lot the house was on, we had two other lots. In 2007 or '08, after the real estate collapse,

Skiff loaded with building materials.
Courtesy of Shelly Somers.

building materials were less expensive, so we decided to build a house on one of the lots. We hauled every bit of the lumber we needed to the island in an outboard boat."

The house is a three-story affair, the second tallest on Rhodes Point. Shelly and Eddie built the house themselves. "We saw a picture of a home in a magazine and patterned the house after that," Shelly said. "The kitchen and living areas are on the middle floor while sleeping areas are on the bottom and top floors. We've thought about moving there after retirement. We could modify the house for retirement, or we may sell it and build another home on our other lot. We don't know what we'll do yet."

The couple has two sons: Justin and Alex. Justin is 27, married, and lives in Alexandria, Virginia. He works in law enforcement. The younger son is Alex. He is 20 and a junior at North Carolina State University studying nuclear engineering. "Although they both enjoy Smith Island, it is unlikely that either of them will return to the area to live," Shelly said.

"We love Smith Island," she continued, describing her feelings for her homeland. "We have a lot of friends over there and we love the activities: fishing, beach combing, collecting arrowheads, hunting, and spending time with my dad. We love the lifestyle over there. There is a closeness among the people. Everybody knows each other and is supportive. There is never a worry about crime; doors are seldom locked. Safety is not an issue; it is a peaceful existence. It would be a great place to retire."

CHAPTER THREE

Jeanie Wilson

"Watching log canoes race is a magnificent sight," says Jeanie Wilson. "Visitors who watch them race are intrigued by them. They've never seen anything like these boats. With their huge, billowing sails propelling them through the water, they are fascinating to look at — and they are fast. A lot of power-boaters find it difficult to keep up with log canoes."

Jeanie Wilson has been involved with the majestic canoes for decades. These vessels have been part of her family for years.

Log canoes are unique to the Chesapeake Bay. Boats of this design don't sail in any other location. Many of the historic vessels had their beginnings well over a hundred years ago. At the turn of the twentieth century, thousands of the majestic vessels plied the waters of the Chesapeake. Today, approximately twenty remain. Practically all of these are listed on the National Register of Historic Places.

Derived from the narrow canoes built by Native Americans, log canoes were carved from huge trees, usually pine, some of which may have been twenty-four inches or more in circumference. Broad axes and burning were used to hollow and shape the hull. Eventually, these skills were passed on to settlers.

Yankee ingenuity saw builders pinning several logs together, thus allowing for a larger craft. Builders hollowed and shaped the logs by hand, with a tool known as an adze. "Most canoes were built from three to five logs," Jeanie stated. "A few, though, were made from seven logs and some of the very large canoes, known as bugeyes, were made from nine logs. Logs of this size aren't available today." Most canoes ranged from twenty-five to thirty-five feet in length.

Until the mid-1900s, the oyster was the major seafood to come from the Bay. The log canoe played a major role in harvesting this succulent bivalve. Chesapeake watermen used canoes to tong for oysters in the shallows of the Bay. Standing on the gunnels of the boat, the waterman would operate the tongs (thin shafts of wood with cage-like appendages attached to their bottoms) in scissor-like fashion in an effort at dislodging the oyster from the depths. Some of these tong shafts could be as long as thirty feet.

"In the 1880s, and hundreds of years before, canoes operated under sail only," Jeanie continued. "They had small sails on them and, back in those days, the first boats to finish their day's work and arrive at the processing plants with their cargo got the highest prices for their catch. Toward the end of the day, processors may have had an adequate supply of oysters and the price they were willing to pay the watermen who came in later was reduced. As a result, it was in the waterman's interest to arrive as early as possible to sell his catch. To make their boats faster, sail areas were increased in size."

For centuries, the reliable canoe served watermen well. In the latter portion of the nineteenth century, when the dredge was introduced to the Chesapeake, the canoe lacked the pulling power to utilize this method of oyster harvesting. Longer and broader canoes, called bugeyes, were built from seven to nine logs in order to pull the heavy dredges. Some of these vessels neared ninety feet in length. The dredge, a four-foot-wide, triangularly shaped iron skeleton with a mesh bag attached to its end, was pulled over the bottom by the boat's momentum as it sailed across the oyster bar.

Later, as the supply of large trees dwindled, boats were built using the plank on frame construction we are familiar with today. The popularity of canoes and bugeyes lessened and eventually died out altogether.

With the advent of the internal combustion engine, the popularity of sail-powered work vessels waned. Many canoes were converted to power shortly after the turn of the twentieth century. Sail rigs were removed and other modifications were made to the boats in order to accommodate the installation of heavy engines.

Purists, however, continued to sail their small log canoes. Impromptu racing became a popular sporting event around the Bay area. "By the 1920s, organized log canoe sail racing had begun," said Jeanie. "Many of the boats that had been converted to power were rigged once again with sails, their engines removed, and the competition began.

"My father-in-law was George H. Wilson. He was known as Captain Bob. He had always enjoyed sailing and was fascinated by log canoes and the J class yachts that competed for the America's Cup (the most prestigious yacht race in the world). He was close friends with brothers C. Lownes Johnson (designer and boat-builder) and Graham Johnson. The three had sailed as crew members on the J class yacht *Rainbow* during the America's Cup competition in 1934. The *Rainbow* was owned by Harold Vanderbuilt.

"Captain Bob was a veteran of World War I, and when he came home he decided to buy a log canoe. Partially, he was motivated to buy a canoe because his future father-in-law, William H. Greene, owned a canoe named *Mary Rider*. The *Mary Rider* won the Governor's Cup three consecutive years, a feat that was not repeated until 1991.

"William H. Greene was born in Australia and his father had been a highly regarded opera singer. Following a move to the United States, he settled on the Eastern Shore, married a local girl, and lived in the town of Claiborne. They lived on an estate named Maple Hall."

In 1923, Capt. Bob purchased a canoe he named *Magic*. He named the boat after an America's Cup contender of the same name that competed in the 1870 races. "He knew the boat was going to do magical things," said Jeanie. Capt. Bob and the Johnson brothers worked on the boat and began racing her in 1925.

Built in 1894 in the backyard of the builder, Charles Tarr, *Magic* was hollowed out of five logs. Tarr lived on historic St. Mary's Square in St. Michaels. A permit from the town was necessary before Tarr was allowed to build the 33'4" boat.

In 1939, *Magic* was shipped to the World's Fair, held that year in Flushing Meadows, New York. "She was cradled and put on a train for the ride to New York," Jeanie said. "When she got to Grand Central Station, she was put on display. I have a picture of the

The *Magic. Courtesy of Jeanie Wilson.*

Magic with the Ziegfeld Girls standing on her deck. John Charles Thomas was a good friend of both Mr. Wilson and Mr. Greene and was instrumental in having the boat appear at the Fair. (Thomas was an opera singer who starred in Broadway musicals, on radio, and acted in silent films. At one point, he was one of the most popular singers in the country). *Magic* was part of the Maryland display at the Fair."

Wilson would race the boat for the next forty years, until 1965. In 1927, he won one of the first organized log canoe races, the prestigious Governor's Cup, at the Miles River Yacht Club in St. Michaels. The Governor's Cup was given to the Miles River Yacht Club by Maryland Governor Albert C. Ritchie. The cup is a perpetual trophy and canoes compete for it annually. The winning boat's name and its owner are inscribed on the trophy; 1927 was the first year the Cup was presented. The *Magic* would go on to win the Cup more often than any other canoe in the fleet that was under the same family ownership.

"In 1965, Capt. Bob turned the boat over to his eldest son, George, Jr., who sailed it until 1970," Jeanie stated. "George, Jr.'s health necessitated that he turn the boat over to his younger brother, Jimmy. Jimmy was my husband and he continued sailing the boat until his death in 2007.

"Following my husband's death, *Magic* went back to George, Jr. His sixteen-year-old grandson, Johnathon Clarke, is now the captain, a position he has had for the last two years. Johnathon is a natural on the tiller. He is just like his uncle Jimmy. He has a good feel for the boat and he's not afraid of her. He gets better every time he races. He almost got a third place last season. He missed it by a margin of only two seconds.

"Johnathon is the fifth generation of the family to sail *Magic*. His mother and father are both on the boat crew, as well as my daughter. His grandfather runs the support boat. It's heartwarming to know that the boat is staying in the family."

Log canoes race every weekend from mid-June until mid-September. Sailing these boats requires a lot of effort. They are complicated and not easily sailed. For the unstable, very narrow boats, remaining upright is a challenge for the skipper and crew.

There are two heavy masts where the gigantic sails are attached. The mast nearest the bow (front) of the boat is referred to as the foresail. The mainsail is located on the mast farther aft and is the smaller of the two. Crews are free to attach a kite atop the mainsail. Kites are smaller sails that resemble sunfish sails, but are much larger. "The kite on the *Jay Dee* (one of the longer boats in the fleet) is larger than *Magic's* mainsail," said Jeanie. "A jib sail, attached to the bow sprit on the front of the boat, rounds out the sail area. These boats carry as much as 1,200 square feet of sail or more."

Because of the narrowness of the canoes and the tremendous sail area, it is necessary to have lots of crew. "The *Jay Dee* carries a minimum of eleven or twelve big men as crew," Jeanie continued. "When there is a lot of wind, she'll carry even more. Smaller boats carry less crew. The *Magic* normally carries a crew of nine or ten. In order to balance the boats, crewmembers shimmy out on fourteen-foot-long hiking boards that hook under the gunnels on the opposite side of the boat. Each boat carries from three to five of these boards. When it is very windy, it is difficult to keep the boats from overturning. The weight of the men riding the hiking boards helps the boat stay upright."

Each sail on a log canoe is controlled by a crewmember. For the mainsail, the sail is controlled from an outrigger attached to the stern (rear) of the boat that overhangs the water. "I used to ride the outrigger," Jeanie said. "I did that off and on for ten or twelve years. One time, we were racing in Cambridge and a storm came up all of a sudden. We turned over when a gust of wind hit us and I got caught underneath the sail. That was one of the scariest times I had while racing."

The unpredictability of Chesapeake weather has, through the years, been a detriment to log canoe sailors. "In August 1963 or '64, we were sailing on the Miles River and a storm

Huge sail area on log canoe.
Courtesy of Jeanie Wilson.

Men on hiking boards.
Courtesy of Jeanie Wilson.

came up quickly," said Jeanie. "To that point, the day had been sunny and pleasant. All of a sudden black clouds rolled in as the boats were headed toward the finish line. The storm and the wind hit about mid-fleet and knocked down all but two of the boats. The *Magic* and one other, I think it was the *Noddy*, were the only boats that finished the race. About five years ago, a similar incident occurred during a race over in Oxford. It was raining so hard you couldn't see your hand in front of you. Another storm hit about two years ago in the Miles River. During each of these storms, one boat remained upright and finished the race."

The start of a log canoe race is chaotic. Boats head for the starting line with full sails drawing. Mass confusion results as the boats jockey back and forth between each other in order to cross the starting line at precisely the moment the clock winds down to zero. The large spectator fleet that follows log canoes is often a hindrance. "There's a mark (buoy) in the Miles River that canoe sailors refer to as the crash mark," Jeanie explained. "When the boats go around that mark, they usually have to jibe (a tricky maneuver that entails swinging the sails from one side of the boat to the other). Canoes are hard to maneuver; they can't turn on a dime. They will weigh from 3,500 to 4,300 pounds. One time Jimmy jibed around the mark and there were two men in a power boat right in front of him. They didn't get out of the way, and when the *Magic* went by them, the hiking boards hit their windshield and knocked it off.

"There used to be a large power boat that came to St. Michaels each day bringing passengers. Invariably, when the canoes were out in the river, the tour boat would pass by them. The boat threw a large wake and, one time when it came through, three canoes capsized. A letter was written to the Coast Guard suggesting that the captain of the tour boat be removed. That captain didn't come back after that as far as I know. When twelve or thirteen people are thrown into the water, there is a possibility of someone getting injured."

Because there is no propulsion in the canoes, each has a support boat, or tender. These are power boats and, like tug boats, they tow the canoes into and out of port before and after racing. Often they are called upon to stand by the canoe after a capsizing has occurred. The narrow, overly canvased canoes frequently capsize during a race. When

Chaotic start of a log canoe race. *Photo by author.*

this happens, sails and masts must be removed and the boat is bailed until it is dry. The support boat then tows the canoe ashore. Their day of racing is usually over following a capsize. It takes great effort to re-rig the vessels and make them race-ready once again.

During many of the years that her husband raced the *Magic*, Jeanie skippered their 38-foot *Boss II* that served as the canoe's chase boat. The *Boss II* was the fourth tender utilized by the *Magic*.

Log canoes are affiliated with yacht clubs and race primarily from four locations: Rock Hall Yacht Club in Rock Hall, Maryland; Miles River Yacht Club in St. Michaels, Maryland; the Tred Avon Yacht Club in Oxford, Maryland; and the Chester River Yacht Club in Chestertown, Maryland. "They have also raced in Annapolis a couple of times in the past," said Jeanie. "These were invitational races."

Twenty-one canoes are currently listed as being eligible to race in the Chesapeake Bay Log Canoe Racing Association. "Some of these canoes are in a state of disrepair," Jeanie stated. "Of the twenty-one that are eligible, fourteen raced for the Governor's Cup in 2011. Canoes race for the Governor's Cup during the initial race of the season held at the Miles River Yacht Club. For the next two races during Governor's Cup weekend, boats are raced in classes. Those that were built prior to 1917 race together in one class for the Sidney Covington Trophy and those built after 1917 race for the John B. Harrison Trophy. Both of these trophies are named in honor of men who built log canoes. These are the only races that split the fleet up like that.

"Every time canoes race they are racing for silver. In addition to the various trophies, canoes race for the honor of being the high point champion for the season. Points are earned for each race sailed. Points are awarded at the finish of each race. The amount of points earned depends on the finishing position of the boat. At the end of the season, the points are totaled and the winning boats are honored. For the 2011 season, the *Island Blossom* was the winner. She has a very consistent crew and they work together very well.

"Boats are assigned a handicap by using a mathematical formula that takes into account several measurements of the boat, the course data, and other factors. As a result of the handicapping system, some boats have to give time to other boats. For example, in a race one boat may finish first by a minute or so before its closest competitors. Because of its handicap, though, it might come in third since it had to give time to two other boats. I am responsible for calculating the handicaps. Assigning handicaps is one of my duties as Secretary/Treasurer of the Chesapeake Bay Log Canoe Racing Association."

Another of Jeanie's duties involves scheduling yearly races. "I start the process in December for the following racing season," she said. "I have to contact the various yacht clubs and get dates that don't conflict; then I send the information out to the owners for feedback. After this, the schedule for the year is released."

Each boat in the Association has a number on its sail. The *Magic's* number is three. "The number on the sail has nothing to do with the age of the boat," Jeanie stated. "In 1971, there was a lottery and each owner drew a number out of a bowl. Jimmy was out of town and I drew for him. I drew number three. It just happens the *Magic* is the third oldest boat in the fleet, but that was only a coincidence."

There are strict rules that govern the racing of log canoes. For example, they cannot be sailed by professional sailors. Each boat is measured for handicapping purposes and adherence to the rules. Both the *Flying Cloud* and the *Jay Dee* had hourglass sterns when they were built. The rules for the Governor's Cup state that boats must have rounded sterns. The *Flying Cloud's* stern was modified so she could compete for the Cup, but the *Jay Dee's* stern was never altered. As a result, she is ineligible to sail for the Governor's Cup.

The *Magic* full-speed ahead.
Courtesy of Jeanie Wilson.

Both Jeanie and her husband were from Talbot County, Maryland. Born in 1943 in Easton, Jeanie has been an Eastern Shoreman for the entirety of her life. "I was born during World War II and they tell me that as I was being delivered there was a blackout throughout the town," she laughed. "My mother and I lived with my grandparents in Oxford for the first six years of my life. Mom remarried when I was six, but I spent a lot of time in Oxford during the summers with my grandparents. My grandfather had a skiff that he prized. He was very protective of that skiff and seldom did he allow anyone else to use it. He let me paddle around in his skiff, though; I felt really special. He also taught me how to dip soft crabs. Oxford was a fun place to live.

"When mom remarried, we moved to St. Michaels and we lived on Chew Avenue. Chew Avenue was a great place to live. It seemed like every house had four or five kids. Mom ended up having five herself.

"Like Oxford, St. Michaels was a great town to grow up in. There was a movie theater, two hotels, two Methodist Churches, a bowling alley, and even a tavern named Deep Blue Sea. On the second floor of the building where the Carpenter Street Saloon is now located, there was a telephone office. The ladies' who worked there wore roller skates to get around the room quickly as the calls came in. My childhood was wholesome and very happy.

"I went to school in St. Michaels and graduated in 1961. There were thirty-six in my graduating class. I played volleyball and field ball in high school. After graduating, I went to work in the office at the Anderson Lumber Co. in Easton.

"I met Jimmy Wilson when I was twelve years old. My uncle, Albert Henckel, was a crewmember on the *Magic* and I liked to watch the races. Jimmy was always around. He and I swam together a lot at the Miles River Yacht Club and he was my dancing partner. We both loved to dance and regardless of who we were dating, we'd always get together and dance whenever we could.

"Jimmy grew up on Leeds Creek. He and I started dating when I was sixteen. One time we took *Magic* out for a sail. Jimmy put me on the tiller and we sailed away from the shore. In a few minutes, he told me to 'bring her up into the wind.' I did and the boat capsized. That could have ended our relationship right then and there. That was the last time I was on the tiller of *Magic*.

"We were married in March 1962 and I had our first daughter in June 1963. A second daughter came along in 1967. One of our daughters crewed on the *Magic* from the time she was ten until she was nineteen. After our marriage, it was full involvement with the *Magic*. Every weekend in the summer was taken up either by working on the boat or going to races. After Jimmy took over, we kept the boat behind our house and did all our own maintenance. We couldn't afford to have professionals do it like many of the other canoe owners.

"When Jimmy first took over the *Magic*, he had a lot to learn. The first season he raced, he capsized nine times out of twenty-four starts. After that season, though, he rarely capsized. He was a natural on the tiller. He knew the boat well and what she would do. He was an excellent sailor."

The *Magic* has won numerous trophies from the Chesapeake Bay Log Canoe Racing Association. George Wilson, Sr. won the Governor's Cup in 1927, the initial year it was given, and again in 1932, 1933, 1949, 1957, and 1960. George H. Wilson, Jr. won the cup in 1963 and 1964. Jimmy Wilson won the cup six times, in 1975, 1977, 1978, 1980, 1981, and 1988.

"Jimmy would go on to win many trophies that were given for the first time," said Jeanie. "In 1988, he won the John C. North Memorial Trophy. The same year, he won the E. Lockwood Hardcastle Memorial Trophy. Jimmy won the Officer's Cup the first time it was awarded in 1994. In 1982, he won the Captain Jack Higgins Cup. In 1990, he won the Miles River Yacht Club's First Gun Trophy and also the Bartlett Cup.

Winning captain and crew, 1990; Jimmy Wilson is in the dark
blue shirt and Jeanie Wilson is left front. *Courtesy of Jeanie Wilson.*

"In 1969, *Magic*, with George H. Wilson, Jr. at the helm, won the Frank B. Lewis Trophy. In 1965, George, Sr. won the Nicols Hardcastle Memorial Trophy. He was runner-up for the high point championship that season.

"Both Capt. Bob and Jimmy have been honored with trophies named in their honor. In 1969, for the first time, the Captain George Wilson, Sr. Trophy was given in his memory and presented to the annual high point champion. The award was given in recognition of his desire and efforts at keeping the log canoes active and racing competitively; *Island Bird* won the trophy the initial year it was given.

"Shortly after Jimmy's death, his friends presented the association with a trophy in his honor. The James H. Wilson Trophy is given annually to the boat that has the most wins during the annual Miles River Yacht Club summer series. It was first awarded in 2007 and won by *Mystery*."

Still active in the Log Canoe Association, Jeanie is present at every race. "I ran the races from 1990 until 2003," she said. "That involved selecting the course, setting the marks (turning points), tallying results, and coordinating activities on the committee boat. Now I go out on *Magic's* tender with my brother-in-law to watch the races.

"I love the thrill of watching the log canoes race," Jeanie stated. "No two races are alike. There's always a story about every individual race. I'm intrigued by log canoes. They are beautiful and historic; I'm thankful to have been a part of their heritage. I guess I'll always be interested and involved with canoes. It's hard to give up something that has been a part of you for over fifty years."

CHAPTER FOUR

Cindy P. Driscoll, DVM

"I was told by my high school guidance counselor to forget any attempt at college," explained Dr. Cindy Driscoll. "Instead, he said I should be satisfied with women's lot in life — having babies. Taken aback by his remarks, I asked to take a vocational test to help identify a career choice. When the results of my test indicated that veterinarian would be a suitable career choice for me, my counselor insisted that I retake the test. He felt the test was inaccurate since 'a woman could never be a veterinarian.' When veterinarian was the result of the retest, he told me I must have done something wrong on the test. 'Just be a secretary,' he said. 'And be happy with your lot in life.'"

Although disillusioned, Cindy harbored no ill feelings toward her counselor. "That's the way things were back in the 1960s," she said. "He was basically a nice man and his beliefs reflected the way things were at the time. He sincerely felt that a woman's place was in the home. Back then I wasn't sure what I could do with the rest of my life. I had always had an interest in animals. My counselor's comments cast a shadow over my dreams and left me confused and wondering about my uncertain future."

Ignoring her counselor's advice, however, Cindy enrolled in college. "My mother encouraged me and felt that I should make an attempt at college," she said. "She thought it would be good if I had a college background for whatever I decided to do in life."

Both of Cindy's older siblings, a brother and sister, were college graduates and had attended nearby Salisbury State College (now Salisbury University), not far from the family's Wicomico County home. Thinking that an education degree was broad in nature and could provide her with a set of skills that would form the basis for a number of career paths, Cindy enrolled in the teacher education program at Salisbury State. "I thoroughly enjoyed the college experience," Cindy explained. "I liked being a college student and, in time, came to realize that my counselor had been totally wrong in his beliefs."

Following her second year of college, Cindy was married to John Driscoll. "I had known John since seventh grade," she said. "I guess I was the pursuer in our relationship.

I'd sit behind him in class and touch his hair and things like seventh graders do. One day, when we were in eighth grade and on a field trip to Philadelphia, I told my cousin that I was going to sit next to John on the bus trip home. I was able to finagle a way to accomplish this and, from then on, we were friends. In tenth grade, we began dating and, after graduating, he went off to St. Mary's College, in the southern part of the state. After one year there, he returned home and joined me at Salisbury State and we were married in 1971.

"John and I have a terrific relationship. In addition to being my husband, he is also my best friend. He has always been very supportive of anything I've wanted to do. I could never have done what I've done if John hadn't been by my side. He's wonderful, funny, and he makes me laugh. We talk a lot; it's amazing that we still do this after forty-two years of marriage."

Awarded the Bachelor of Science degree in 1973 with a major in psychology, the following year John enrolled at Towson University to work toward an advanced degree. For two years, while earning credits toward a masters in psychology, the couple lived in a dormitory at the University of Maryland Baltimore County, in Catonsville, where they were resident directors (house parents).

After John earned his master's degree, the Driscolls moved to Mississippi, where he enrolled in the Ph.D. program at the University of Southern Mississippi. Cindy and John were in Mississippi for two years. They worked as residential directors in a campus dormitory and Cindy also did clerical work in the housing office.

"While in Mississippi, I decided that I wanted to work with animals," said Cindy. "Since a little girl, I had always loved dogs and cats. I always liked being outdoors, looking at wildlife, and thought that working with animals might make a rewarding career. I visited an academic/guidance counselor at Southern Mississippi and asked him where I could go for veterinary training. He cautioned me that because there were few veterinary schools (less than twenty at that time) that it was easier to get into medical school than veterinary school. He was also pessimistic about the possibility of a woman becoming a veterinarian. He suggested that I contact the schools to determine their entry requirements. Maryland did not have a veterinary school at that time, but had contracts with four colleges as a reciprocal agreement and established in-state tuition for those schools. I contacted each of the schools to learn of their entrance requirements."

After John earned his doctorate, he joined a clinical psychology practice in Severna Park and the Driscolls moved to Bowie, Maryland. Over the next two years, Cindy took courses at Bowie State College and the University of Maryland. She concentrated her studies in the area of science because these were courses she hadn't taken while an undergraduate student at Salisbury. She earned sixty credits during those years. While at the University of Maryland, she took courses in the animal sciences department and gained

Cindy's first exposure to outdoor life was fishing with her dad. *Courtesy of Dr. C. Driscoll.*

"I asked for a doctor's kit for Christmas."
Courtesy of Dr. C. Driscoll.

experience at a small animal veterinary practice. One of her instructors became her pre-vet advisor.

"Dr. Kathy Nepote was encouraging and very supportive," said Cindy. "She suggested that I get experience working with large and small animals. For two years, I worked in a small animal hospital to gain experience. This was rewarding, and I especially enjoyed interacting with the owners of pets that were brought into the facility. To gain experience with large animals, I worked at a large dairy farm for several months. It was the last working dairy farm in Prince George's County. I worked there a few mornings each week, beginning at 4:30 a.m. A gentleman named Mr. Tom Wilson operated the dairy farm. I also devoted a day each week to working with a vet who specialized in equine medicine and I also worked with cattle. As a child, I was thrown by a horse and, as a result, I never felt comfortable working with large animals." As Cindy juggled all these activities, she also worked part-time as a clerk in the architectural office at the University of Maryland.

Dr. Nepote also encouraged Cindy to get experience in the field of research. "As I commuted to the University of Maryland, I passed the Patuxent Research Center," Cindy explained. "I called them and asked if there were any activities I could get involved with at the Center in order to gain research experience. They suggested that I visit the facility and talk with their veterinarian. I went to the Center and spoke with Dr. Jim Carpenter. During our discussion and tour of the facility, I found that it was actually the Patuxent Wildlife Research Center and that they worked with threatened and endangered species. During that visit, it was as though the sun came out and rainbows appeared in the sky. The birds sang and I had an epiphany. I knew that working with endangered and threatened species was what I wanted to do for my life's work. The environmental movement had begun in the '70s and '80s, and I wanted to be a part of protecting the environment. Working with protected species and wildlife seemed a perfect fit. I worked with Dr. Carpenter for two years beginning in 1981 and never looked back."

Mentored by Dr. Carpenter, Cindy worked with endangered species like the masked bob-white quail, whooping cranes, condors, and bald eagles. "We even raised chicks to fledging, manipulated the environment of adult birds to see how they adapted," she said. "It was amazing! I was thrilled to be part of the research effort and felt very lucky to have that opportunity. The people were very nice and I felt like that's where I belonged."

Armed with the credits and experiences gained in the field, Cindy applied and was accepted into the veterinary program at the Virginia-Maryland Regional College of Veterinary Medicine on the campus of Virginia Tech in Blacksburg, Virginia, and began her studies in 1983. "I wanted to study wildlife, but, unfortunately, this was not available at the time," said Cindy. "Veterinary schools depend on funding from the private sector and no funding for studying wildlife was streaming into the school. However, during my first year I was accepted as a summer Research Fellow in the VMRCVM Toxicology Department. Dr. Marian Ehrich, another amazing mentor, advised me to go one step further and publish two papers on mitigating the effects of mycotoxins in animal feeds. We also worked with chickens in an attempt to prevent a decrease in production of poultry. I learned to be regimented and organized in my research methods with Dr. Ehrich."

Being that far away from home was difficult for the Driscolls. During their four years in Blacksburg, Cindy's father died, as did John's mother. His brother also died during those years. "In many ways, it was a very difficult time in our lives," said Cindy.

In 1987, Cindy was awarded the DVM (Doctor of Veterinary Medicine) degree. "My wonderful husband, in the summer of 1987, announced that he had a graduation gift for me," Cindy said. "He had been saving for years and had put money aside. He told me he'd take me anywhere in the world. We went to Great Britain for two weeks. It was a complete surprise and we had a remarkable time."

Returning to the Eastern Shore, the Driscolls and their eight dogs settled in Centreville, a small town not far from the Chesapeake Bay Bridge. Cindy's first job, after earning her DVM degree, was at an Eastern Shore toxicology laboratory. She was the laboratory supervisor and supervised biologists who worked in the lab. She conducted necropsy studies (autopsies) on animals to assess the effects of agricultural chemical products on wildlife. While employed there, she was asked to work on toxicology issues of fish in the Chesapeake Bay. Because she had no experience working with fish in veterinary school, she went to the Cooperative Oxford Laboratory (COL) in Oxford, Maryland, for training.

The Oxford Laboratory is a joint effort between state and federal governments: The Maryland Department of Natural Resources (MD DNR) and NOAA (National Oceanic and Atmospheric Association). Originally conceived in the 1960s to study diseases in oyster and other shellfish populations in the Chesapeake and Delaware Bays, the lab was eventually expanded to include studies in fisheries. Currently, one of the primary activities of the lab is monitoring land-based activities that may negatively impact animals that live along the Chesapeake watershed.

Cindy learned a lot from the scientists at the lab and thoroughly enjoyed her experiences. "I was asked to develop a stranding response program for marine mammals and sea turtles," she explained. "In the late 1980s, dolphins stranded themselves on beaches and died for no apparent reason. There was interest in finding out why these strandings occurred. My veterinary training served me well, but I had no experience with these protected species. To gain knowledge of dolphin anatomy, I was fortunate to receive training at the Smithsonian Institution in Washington, D.C. Dr. Jim Mead and Charley Potter were incredible mentors; they conducted necropsies and examined every tissue of marine mammals. I worked beside these amazing scientists for two weeks. I became familiar with dolphin anatomy as a result and eventually became proficient with the anatomy of all marine mammals that frequent our shores, even whales. Our stranding program was developed in conjunction with the Smithsonian, the National Aquarium, adjoining states, and partners assisting and volunteering with us.

"Ultimately, I was invited to work at NOAA in their Silver Spring, Maryland, office, full-time in 1992. My work involved policy issues, scientific research, and national stranding program development. I was there for six years, until 1998. I was, however, office bound and, although it was rewarding, I preferred field work over policy work in an office building. My office was a long commute from Centreville. By then, John and I had a young school-age daughter, Caitlan, who was very busy with piano lessons, dance, sports, and other activities. Since John's job required evening hours, if I got home late, she sometimes did not get to participate in those activities."

Cindy began talking to folks at the state level about a permanent position with MD DNR while she was at the Oxford Lab. There had never been a state fish and wildlife veterinarian at the Department of Natural Resources in Maryland. In 1999, she was appointed to the position of State Fish and Wildlife Veterinarian for the Maryland Department of Natural Resources. Her office was based at the Oxford Lab.

At COL, she developed a framework for not only aquatic wildlife response, but also terrestrial animal health investigation. "It seems like everywhere I've worked I've developed my own program," explained Cindy. "After developing the stranding program for MD DNR, then the national program for NOAA, I developed the Fish and Wildlife Health Program for the state. Lots of coordination went into formulating the program. Coordination between a variety of state and federal organizations and agencies had to occur. Designing and implementing the program has been exciting and rewarding." Cindy has been based in Oxford ever since.

In the late '90s and early 2000s, Cindy and her colleagues investigated fish kills in the Pocomoke and other Chesapeake rivers. They also looked at fish kills in North Carolina and worked with biologists throughout the mid-Atlantic region. Menhaden were reportedly affected with a condition thought to be Pfiesteria. As with all investigations, this fish kill was conducted methodically and the fish were found to have fungal bacterial and parasitic lesions. They also developed a project to investigate mycobacterial lesions in rockfish and found that most diseases were temperature and salinity dependent. "We can't do much about these things because we can't alter these conditions in the entire Chesapeake region," said Cindy. "However, we now know a lot more about disease prevalence than we did previously."

In addition to marine mammals, Cindy also investigates threatened and endangered sea turtles. The process is similar to the response efforts for dolphins, whales, and seals. Loggerheads are the primary species that strand along our coasts, although some Kemp's Ridleys (the most endangered sea turtle species) and leatherbacks (the largest sea turtle) strand in Maryland. All are protected under federal and state laws. Over the years, there were anecdotal reports of sea turtles nesting on the northern end of Assateague Island.

"Most sea turtles are either on the endangered or threatened list," Cindy explained. "This past July (2012) we heard that a loggerhead turtle had nested on the island. Loggerheads are huge sea turtles, some of them might measure three to four feet across and weigh three hundred pounds. We went down there with representatives from the National Aquarium in Baltimore and the Stranding Coordinator from the National Park Service. We decided to excavate the nest because it was way past time when the eggs should have hatched. Hurricane Sandy was also bearing down on the coast and we feared the storm might also destroy the eggs. As we began excavating, we found that there were live hatchlings. We were amazed. It was beyond the number of days for incubation to occur and the temperature was not right for that to happen. Nobody expected that. The hatchlings were taken to the National Aquarium in Baltimore. One of the hatchlings is still alive. It was shipped to an aquarium in North Carolina. Eventually, it will be released back into the wild. We've also documented leatherback strandings in Maryland, in the Chesapeake. The turtles have been sighted as far north as the Chester River."

In 2000, the Oxford lab received a federal grant under the Endangered Species Act to study sea turtles and short nose sturgeon. For many years sturgeon were fished in the

Bay. Sturgeon were valued as a source for caviar. They date from pre-historic times and were hunted very nearly to extinction. Under Cindy's supervision, the sturgeon project was developed and implemented. Because the sturgeon supply was less than adequate in the Chesapeake, scientists traveled to nearby Delaware Bay for their investigations. They found that many were intersex fish; males were becoming female and a few were turning from female to male. The team concluded that this was occurring because of pollutants in the water. Sexual oddities in other fish species have also been reported.

The other portion of the project investigated sea turtles as they were found in watermen's pound nets. Scientists from the lab went out with watermen as they harvested their nets and tagged sea turtles, weighed, measured, and took blood samples. They were released afterwards. The sea turtle project ended in 2007-08. "The goal of the project was to become familiar with the size and type of turtles and to track what habitat they use," said Cindy. "We were also interested in their health. This project resulted from the development of our MD Conservation Plan for Sea Turtles, Mammals and Shortnosed Sturgeon and from our hope to work with watermen when these animals are present."

In October 1990, a large, three-hundred-pound female bottlenose dolphin was found dead in Tuckahoe State Park, located on a tributary of the Choptank River. Although dolphins are common in the Bay during warmer months, Cindy and her colleagues knew that it had become disoriented to be that far from the main waters of the Bay. The huge dolphin was so heavy that it had to be cut into thirds in order to get it out of the water and back to the lab for examination. The skeletal remains are at the VA-MD Regional College of Veterinary Medicine in Blacksburg, Virginia.

Pfiesteria fish sampling, 1997. *Courtesy of Dr. C. Driscoll.*

Dolphin and porpoise strandings are common in the Chesapeake. "Already this year (2013) there have been fourteen reports of strandings," Cindy stated. "Most of these have been dolphins. There was a report just last week of a dolphin stranding on Hooper's Island. We are also aware of a reported stranding on Smith Island.

"Our studies investigate why strandings occur. We are interested in the time of year and which species strand. We look for patterns and trends. We know that many species, like dolphin, enter the Chesapeake following a food supply. They chase fish into the Bay and are reported to range pretty far north. Every year there are dolphin sightings in the Choptank River. We've also received sightings of seals in the Bay.

"A couple of years ago we received a report that a large black and white adult harp seal was seen on a private dock outside Baltimore. It should not have been in the Bay, but it was and it appeared healthy and doing well. Stranding responders from the National Aquarium monitored the seal for a day or so. The seal finally left on its own."

In 1990, a 65-ton whale was speared by the bow of an oceangoing tanker. "It ended up in Curtis Bay," said Cindy. "Charley Potter of the Smithsonian, Division of Mammals was on-site and collected skeletal specimens with the help of state and aquarium officials. At the end of the day, several of us piled into my husband's brand new car for the trip back home. We kept that car for twelve years and 330,000 miles and never completely got the smell of decomposing whale blubber out of it. Although we had it washed, detailed, and disinfected, the 'aroma' never completely left."

About twenty years ago, Cindy received a report that a whale sighting had occurred near the Chesapeake Bay Bridge. Several people had taken photos of the whale. "It was

Conducting necropsy examination on a whale.
Courtesy of Dr. C. Driscoll.

a humpback and it seemed to be normal and healthy," she said. "It was lunge feeding for fish around the bridge. In lunge feeding, the whale feeds by surfacing underneath a school of fish. That was one of the very first times a live whale was documented in the Chesapeake Bay."

In 1994, a call was received from someone in the Upper Bay who reported a manatee sighting in the Susquehanna River. "We were skeptical of seeing a manatee that far north and asked if perhaps the person had seen a log instead of a manatee," said Cindy. "A week later two different people reported sightings in the Elk and Sassafras Rivers. We investigated and found that the sightings were legitimate. A year before, a manatee sighting had been reported in the state of Virginia. Within a few weeks, additional sightings were reported. In September, a sighting was reported in the Chester River and in October we caught the manatee that we named 'Chessie' near Queenstown.

"We took him to the National Aquarium, where he stayed for a couple of days. We then flew him to Sea World in Florida. The folks at Sea World, U.S. Fish and Wildlife, and the State of Florida tagged him and attached a satellite transmitter. He was released into the Indian River. The following year 'Chessie' again appeared in the Chesapeake Bay. He also put in an appearance in Connecticut and Rhode Island. We had proven that manatees do, indeed, range as far north as New England. We get reports of manatee sightings every year in our area. Every couple of years we get a report that our 'Chessie' is once again visiting us.

"In 2010, we received word that a dead manatee was found in the Patuxent River. Our necropsy examination found that this animal was known to population researchers by the scars on its back and flukes and had been spotted in Virginia waters in the fall. We believe that this animal died from cold-shock when it failed to head back to Florida. Manatees travel up the Intra Coastal Waterway from Florida. We have been told that Capt. John Smith reported seeing manatees in the Chesapeake during his explorations in the 1600s."

Not only does Cindy work with animals that are directly linked to the Chesapeake, she also works with more recognizable species. She has investigated health and disease in a variety of species. Some of the diseases investigated include Avian Influenza, Newcastle Disease Virus, West Nile Virus in birds, and Chronic Wasting Disease in deer.

Health assessment studies have included sampling black bears since their numbers are increasing in the western counties of Maryland. Three collaborative journal articles will be published in 2013: one on Trichinella and Toxoplasmosis in bears, another on black bear disease exposure testing results, and the third on a massive bird die-off on Poplar Island in 2012.

Brown Pelicans have been migrating further north in recent years. "They have been nesting on Holland Island since 1987," Cindy said. "Holland Island, located near

Conducting black bear assessment and cub tagging.
Courtesy of Dr. C. Driscoll.

Sampling a pelican chick on Holland's Island.
Courtesy of Dr. C. Driscoll.

the southern boundary of Dorchester County, hosts a large colony of pelicans each summer. Our wildlife biologists band chicks each year and I examine and take biological samples from them. They look good, very healthy, and they are doing quite well. About five years ago, however, we received word that some of the chicks did not migrate south and were remaining in St. Mary's County. We believe they stayed because well-meaning residents were feeding them. Approximately fifty died and many of the remaining chicks suffered from frostbite."

Cindy's work has also taken her far beyond the shores of the Bay. She has ventured as far as Alaska to work with sled dogs involved in the Yukon Quest Race and annually visits the Cayman Islands as part of the Marvet training program. In the Cayman's she is a faculty member training young veterinarians in marine mammal science. Similarly, she is a faculty member of the AquaVet Program in Woods Hole, Massachusetts, where she also assists in training veterinary students.

Cindy enjoys interacting with students. "I teach an evening course at the University of Maryland in the animal science department," she explained. "It's rewarding to show them there is another aspect of veterinary medicine besides dogs, cats, horses, and cows. Many of them don't realize that we are also involved with wildlife."

Another new effort involves collaboration with state agency veterinarians in the agriculture and health departments. The *MD One Health Bulletin* was developed

Conducting health assessment and taking samples for analysis. *Courtesy of Dr. C. Driscoll.*

to inform Maryland veterinarians about significant diseases and issues occurring in the state. It is distributed not only to veterinarians, but also to health and agriculture department staff members and wildlife biologists. Recently, other states have adopted the bulletin for their own use.

Through the years, Dr. Driscoll has received many awards and recognitions for her work. She was presented a merit award for her efforts from the U. S. Fish and Wildlife Service. While in veterinary school, she was awarded the David Bogash Award for being the student who demonstrated the most compassion among her peers. The faculty, as well as her fellow students, selected her for this award. Her career has been highlighted in the newsletters of the American Association of Wildlife Veterinarians and the *Wildlife Disease News Digest*. These publications have identified Dr. Driscoll as a veterinarian who has made a difference. She served on the Committee on Environmental Issues for the American Veterinary Medical Association and is a member of several committees within the Wildlife Disease Association. For six years, she was a member of the Board of Directors of the International Association of Aquatic Animals.

"My most important awards, though, are my husband and daughter," said Cindy. "Their constant caring and dedication have been inspirational to me. Caitlan is now twenty-three and is absolutely wonderful. She graduated from the University of Delaware with a double major in Apparel Design and Mass Communications, had an internship in New York City, and later came home and started her own business with a friend. We are very close. It is great having a daughter and husband that are both very understanding and encouraging. This has allowed me to pursue my amazing career."

An advocate for a cleaner environment, she understands well the implications for the Chesapeake Bay if changes are not forthcoming. "We are all stewards of the environment and the animals that surround us," she said.

CHAPTER FIVE

Mary Ada Marshall

"Around here they call me the cake lady," said Mary Ada Marshall of Smith Island, Maryland's only inhabited offshore island. Tylerton, one of three communities on the island, is the place Mary Ada calls home.

With a full-time population of fifty-one, Tylerton sits on land scarcely above sea level. Approaching the town requires a trip through waterways surrounded by lush marshes and wetlands. A variety of wildlife welcomes the visitor to the lovely hamlet surrounded by the blue-green waters of the Chesapeake.

"I was born over in Ewell," she said. "I was named after both my grandmothers. Mine is the fourth or fifth generation to live on Smith Island. There were six of us kids. I was the first girl following three brothers. One of my brothers died when he was six months old. I'm told that after he was embalmed, he broke out with the measles. They say that happens a lot. Another brother died when he was 21. His boat exploded while he was in it. He'd only been married for two years. That was in 1975; it was a very sad time, it liked to killed my mom and dad."

Mary Ada's marriage to a Tylerton man, Dwight Marshall, necessitated her relocation to that village. "I've been over here ever since," she said. "I met Dwight on the school boat. We'd travel to the mainland to attend secondary schools over in Crisfield."

A lot of changes to island life have occurred during Mary Ada's years of living there. "When I was growing up, there were over six hundred people living on the island," she continued. "A few years ago, we had so many kids coming up in Tylerton that we had our own school. The school had three grades in each room and students didn't leave that classroom all day. They stayed with the same teacher for six years of grade school. That teacher really got to know her students and the students also knew her well by the time the school year was over. In the end, we only had three kids in the school and it was closed down. Eventually, the school was sold. It is now a private residence. People from Pennsylvania bought it. They visit the island occasionally."

Smith Island Marsh. *Photo by author.*

Elementary students now ride an inter-island boat to attend school in Ewell, about two miles away. "It's funny that our Tylerton School was closed for lack of enrollment," the sprightly Mary Ada laughed. "Nowadays we have five kids going over to Ewell everyday for school. There are only seven or eight students in the school altogether and now the majority is from Tylerton. Students go there for grades pre-K till grade seven. For high school, students travel to the mainland everyday on a high-speed, $600,000 catamaran with heat and air-conditioning. They go to Crisfield High School.

Tylerton entry. *Photo by author.*

Former school building. *Photo by author.*

"When I was coming up, the county paid for us to stay with a family in Crisfield. We'd go over to Crisfield on Monday morning and stay till Friday afternoon, when the passenger boat would take us back to Smith Island. We'd get $4 a week as an allowance. From that, we'd have to save 25 cents to pay the taxi to get us back to the boat on Friday afternoons. We'd always save 50 cents to go to the movies. We'd walk downtown and attend the movie. We thought that was the greatest thing since sliced bread. In addition to the $4, my grandmother would give me an extra dollar each week. I thought I was as rich as Donald Trump."

Mary Ada graduated from high school in 1965. "Very few island kids went to college in those days," she said. "We just didn't have the money, families couldn't afford it. Two of my four children went to college, though; our daughter, Maria, graduated from Washington College in Chestertown and Dwight Jr. (Duke), one of our three sons, graduated from Salisbury University. He's never married...he married his briefcase. He's in the insurance business in Salisbury and sits on the Board at the University. My daughter works on Capitol Hill. Colin Powell's son is the CEO of the company where she works. My other sons are Kevin and Jamie. Kevin is a welder, a mighty fine one at that. He built his own aluminum boat. She's out there at the dock. Jamie is in law enforcement. All my kids have done well, I'm very fortunate."

When Mary Ada was growing up, young island children were only familiar with children in their own villages. "We didn't know any kids from the other communities unless they were relatives," she said. "Only after we were older did we socialize with kids from away."

Later, as island youngsters reached the age of thirteen, dances were held each Saturday evening in the fire hall. In Ewell, the fire hall had a jukebox and teens would gather there for a sock hop. Rhodes Point and Tylerton boys would come to Ewell to attend the sock hops. "We got to know a lot of the boys from the other areas that way," said Mary Ada. "In fact, lots of Ewell girls married Tylerton boys they met at the sock hops."

Only six teenagers live on Smith Island presently. There were twenty-six island children in Mary Ada's class alone as she went through school. "Our island population is getting older," she stated. "Half the people living in Tylerton now are age seventy and older. Our people are aging out. There aren't many young people coming up. The young ones are moving off island to find decent employment. They can't make a living working out on the Bay. The water business is slow now. There are so many rules and regulations imposed by the state. If watermen keep getting pounded on, there won't be any left. I ask Dwight, 'what're we going to do — pick up and leave?' He says he's not budging until the Lord tells him to. I guess I'm right there with him, but you do have all this in the back of your mind. I don't want to leave the island because this is home. We've worked our whole lives to get what we have. Have we done it all in vain? This is where my children were raised and where my grandkids visit. I just don't know…"

Mary Ada's grandchildren visit the island frequently and enjoy their time there. "They go out and play on the docks and have a good time," she said. "One day, one of them came to me and asked if he could have my house after I die. I said, 'My Lord, do you want me to die?' He said no, that he was just thinking ahead of time. I said, 'What about my children?' He said that they've all got houses, they don't need another one. I thought that was kind of cute."

Growing up in Ewell, Mary Ada seldom left the island. "Every year at Labor Day we'd go to Crisfield and attend the Crab Derby," she said. "We'd spend the day there. There was a little store on Main Street where we'd go and buy our school supplies for the coming year. We'd get a pencil box, crayons, and other items, and then we'd watch the parade and come on home. We'd be so happy. You'd think we'd been on a trip to Manhattan or someplace, we'd be so excited. It didn't take a whole lot to content us, I had a good childhood."

Every summer Mary Ada and her family would take a day trip to Ocean City, Maryland's only ocean resort. "I thought that was the greatest thing in the world," she explained. "We'd look forward to that trip all year. About thirty of us would go. We'd hire a school bus to take us once we got on the mainland. We'd go down there and have a lot of fun; come back all sunburned with big hats, cotton candy, and popcorn. We thought that was the greatest thing there ever was. On one trip one of the boys hollered out as we passed a large building, 'Look, there's a large Tabernacle.' He was looking at a chicken house. The whole bus cracked up laughing."

Kids in those days seemed to be more appreciative than they are now, Mary Ada feels. "We were appreciative of everything our parents did for us," she stated. "One time I was getting ready to attend a prom at school and needed a gown. I had been chosen Valentine Princess. You'd think I had been appointed the Queen of Sheba or something. We went off island to Salisbury looking for a prom gown. Daddy kept a car in Crisfield and, on the way home, we had a flat tire. It was cold and the roads were icy. I looked out and daddy had ice forming on his hat as he worked on the car. After we were on our way again, I said to him, 'Daddy, I want you to know how much I appreciate your buying me this pretty dress and all the trouble you've gone through to get it.' He looked at me and said, 'Darling, you're worth all that effort to me.' I'll never forget that day.

It wasn't the material things that mattered; it was all he had gone through that day to get the dress for me. I don't know if kids today are appreciative like that. Now, island kids have their own cars in Crisfield. They have their iPods, computers, and everything you can think of."

Electricity came to the island in 1949. About five years later, telephone service arrived. "I remember when we got our first TV set," Mary Ada smiled. "It was a great big square box and we had an antenna on the roof. We thought that was high tech. The telephone had a rotary dial. We enjoyed talking to our friends on the telephone. Today kids send text messages to each other, sometimes while they're in the same room."

Religion is an important part of island life. Methodism is the only religion practiced on the island. Each village supports its own Methodist church. "Everybody on Sunday would go to Church," she continued. "My grandmother thought that Sunday was only for Church, no work was to be done on the Sabbath. She thought that if you went so far as to pick up a pair of scissors on Sunday the Devil would get you. You weren't supposed to do anything resembling work on that day.

"We still go to church on Sunday; we listen to the message and testimonials. We pay attention to the Bible. Pastor Rick comes over every Sunday and gives us the Word. We've always pulled together on the island. That's what life's all about. It's not about gathering up a collection of worldly things that don't amount to a row of pins. It's what's in your heart that matters."

Christmastime is very special on Tylerton. Mary Ada explained that Tylerton is one of the prettiest villages anywhere at Christmastime. "Christmas lights are everywhere," she said. "Residents decorate their porches, outside trees, shrubbery. They put candles in every window. Anything you could wrap a light around is lighted. The village looks like a Norman Rockwell painting, it's that pretty. The church is exquisitely beautiful.

"I remember the first Christmas Dwight and I were married. We were over to my parents' home in Ewell. There were twenty-some people gathered there. It was Christmas Eve and it started to snow. It was a beautiful sight."

During the Christmas season, each of the three island churches rotates as host church for a Christmas party. "The United Methodist Women put on the party," Mary Ada continued. "Lots of women who have moved off island come back to attend the party. It's the most fun; I guess we've had one hundred women at the party. After we eat, we have entertainment. Some of the funniest jokes and skits are performed. Everybody dresses in their Christmas finery. Before all that happens, we have a religious service in the Sanctuary. We've been doing this for twenty years or more."

None of the villages on Smith Island are incorporated. Tylerton, however, has a community council made up of community leaders. Although the council is informal, many important issues are discussed. Occasionally, the minister of the church is requested to appear at council meetings to assist with decisions.

Villagers in each community exhibit their own characteristic accents, according to Mary Ada. "We talk different than they do over in Ewell or Rhodes Point," she laughed. "The Elizabethan twang is different in each community."

Tylerton has its own post office. Mail is delivered to the Ewell Post Office and, subsequently, ferried over to Tylerton.

Women, according to Mary Ada, are a very active part of the community. United Methodist Women make dresses for Haitian girls. Just last year, over one hundred dresses were shipped away from the island. Currently, women are making pillows for breast cancer patients. "The outreach programs here are unbelievable," she said.

Weather is a constant concern for island residents. "My great-grandmother was a prayerful woman," Mary Ada said, shaking her head. "There were about twenty skipjacks

Tylerton United Methodist Church.
Photo by author.

Tylerton Post Office. *Photo by author.*

based on Smith Island in those days. It was back in the 1930s, just before Christmas. Word went out that the skipjacks couldn't get home because of ice in the Bay. Their masts were visible in the distance, but they were jammed in by the ice. My great-grandmother, after finding out about the skipjacks, went upstairs to her room and prayed and prayed and prayed. She came downstairs and told everybody to get the word out that the men on the skipjacks were going to be all right. A little wind came up and the ice parted enough for the boats to go on through. Every boat got in safely and the men came home for Christmas. After they got in, the harbor iced in again and the skipjacks didn't get out again until March. My great-grandmother was a remarkable woman."

A few years ago, a family was heading home to Smith Island following a shopping trip to the mainland. "Coming across Tangier Sound, one of the planks came off the boat," Mary Ada explained. "They sent out a distress call, but the boat went down. A couple of men from the island went out and found them — they were able to save the whole family. The water swallowed up the boat in an instant. Not even an oil slick was found. No sign of the groceries or anything else that was aboard the boat was ever found. Those people were saved by a minute. I think they had a guardian angel looking out for them."

More recently, the Bay froze, limiting accessibility to the island. "In 1975 or '76, ice was everywhere," Mary Ada stated. "We could look out in the Bay and see icebergs as tall as our houses. We were froze in for six or eight weeks. We'd get our mail and food supplies by helicopter. Now and then, the helicopter would take a couple of passengers to the mainland. My son, Duke, had cut his lip real bad and needed stitches. He and I flew in the helicopter to get to the doctor. Heating oil was flown over in big drums hanging from cables under the helicopter. The state has always been supportive and helpful, but it's worrisome when the weather gets like that. It's especially hard on the old people."

Weather added excitement as Mary Ada was readying for the birth of her daughter. "The wind was blowing fifty miles an hour," she stated. "I knew if we didn't get help soon the baby and I would be in big trouble. I called Dwight and told him I had to get to Crisfield to the hospital. We went across Tangier Sound in the middle of a thunderstorm. We really got jolted around, it was very rough. We'd called ahead and an ambulance was waiting for us. Maria was born just one hour after we got to Crisfield.

"We've had babies born on the way over to the hospital and some are born at home. A helicopter will come if it's an emergency. My grandson was born after his mother was taken off by helicopter because there was so much ice in the Sound that the boats couldn't get through."

Tropical Storm Sandy brushed by the island recently. "We didn't evacuate," said Mary Ada. "They weren't calling for that much wind, but it turned into a super storm. Crisfield really took it on the nose. The tide was bottlenecked there and the storm surge caused a lot of flooding and damage. It took out a lot of the low-lying houses.

"Rhodes Point, being the furthest westward of the villages, is worse off than we are when we get a bad storm. They are right on the Bay. The Bay side is much rougher than the Tangier side where we are. When high winds and high tides come, they undermine their roads and shanties."

In the spring of each year, the church has a special service for watermen, past and present, of Smith Island. A moving portion of the service is the tolling of the bell for those who have been lost at sea. In 2013, the ceremony honored the memory of thirty-three Smith Island men who have lost their lives on the surrounding waters of the Chesapeake Bay.

Medical care comes to each of the island villages by way of a nurse practitioner. She visits each community once a month. A few generations ago a doctor lived in Ewell. The doctor delivered babies in his home. "I was born there," said Mary Ada. "The doctor's office was in the cellar of his house and that's where the babies were born. There were beds down there for the mothers and they'd stay there for a week or so after the birth."

Mary Ada is, perhaps, best known for her renditions of Smith Island cake. Smith Island cakes are massive, with thin layers of cake separated by generous proportions of icing. "I've seen cakes with as many as sixteen layers," she said. "Most of mine are eight layers, though."

Tales of the origin of Smith Island cakes are varied. "There's always been layered cakes on Smith Island," she said. "Ladies always made three and four layered cakes. One time there was a cake walk on the island at Halloween time to raise money for the school. For cake walks, a big circle was drawn on the floor and a smaller circle was drawn inside it. Numbers were placed between the circles, sort of like numbers on a clock face. Music was put on a record player and people would walk between the lines of the circle. A woman would stand in the middle of the circle holding a cake. When the music was stopped, a number was called out and the person standing closest to that number won the cake.

"One year they didn't have enough cakes for the cake walk so they cut them in half in order to get a better supply. When they cut one cake in half, it had six or seven layers. We don't know who made that cake, but it became a contest after that to see who could bake a cake with the most layers. That was the beginning of the Smith Island cake."

Tourism officials became interested in Smith Island cakes as a way to publicize Somerset County and Smith Island. "They felt that would be good for the island," said Mary Ada. "They thought everybody who came to the island would want some of the cake when they visited."

Eventually, with the help of tourism organizations, Smith Island cake came to the attention of Maryland's governing body, the General Assembly. "We went up to Annapolis six times, we must have taken a ton of cakes up there," Mary Ada continued. "We were there in 2008 when the Legislature passed a bill making Smith Island cake the state dessert. I was at the bill signing with the Governor. That was a thrill; never in my wildest dreams did I ever think I'd be a part of something like that."

In 2008, Mary Ada was given the Heritage Interpreter Award by Lower Eastern Shore Heritage in honor of her efforts at having Smith Island cake named the state dessert. Articles in a variety of newspapers have also been written about Mary Ada. *Saveur Magazine* did a spread called "8 Story Glory." A group from Japan came to the island and filmed her making a cake. Mary Ada has also appeared on TV. "I remember one time I was on my way to Baltimore for an appearance on the *Marty Bass Show*," she laughed. "I was very sick with kidney stones. All that recognition and attention sold a lot of cakes."

Mary Ada's husband, Dwight, has also enjoyed recognition for his efforts. He has won many boat docking contests for his prowess in boat handling. He and his son, Kevin, were featured in the June 1993 issue of *National Geographic* magazine.

Mary Ada comes from a long line of women who enjoy cooking. "I guess cooking is in my genes," she said. "I learned to make Smith Island cakes watching my mother and grandmother. My grandmother cooked for camp meetings on the island. There were no

Mary Ada's Smith Island cake. *Photo by author.*

restaurants on the island in those days. My grandmother and grandfather would literally move into the church basement to prepare for the camp meetings. Boatloads of people would come; camp meetings lasted all week. Hundreds came by boat, and just about everybody on the island attended the meetings also. One year we had a special guest. He came in by helicopter. It was Brooks Robinson of the Baltimore Orioles. I had the privilege of serving him and got his autograph. It's been a busy life, but a good one."

One store is located in Tylerton. In addition to groceries, the store also prepares sandwiches, etc. "I make crab cakes for the store," said Mary Ada. "My son, Duke, owns the store. Although he lives in Salisbury, he is very active in sending supplies over to the island. Twice a week he does that. He doesn't make much money from the store, but he realizes that if there was no store, the village would have a difficult time surviving. The store gives visitors a place where they can eat and it gives the boat captains a little extra money hauling groceries to the island."

Anthony Bourdain, of the Travel channel, came to the island and filmed a segment with Mary Ada. "He came over here in forty-mile-an-hour winds," she said. "It was very rough that day. We showed him around the village. He watched as crabs were steamed and picked. He also watched us make the meat up into crab cakes. Later, when he bit into a crab cake, he said it was worth every high sea he had to go through to get over here."

The Chesapeake Bay Foundation (CBF) has a center in Tylerton. School students visit the center for three-day stretches. Students involve themselves with nature studies that focus on the health of the Chesapeake Bay. By visiting the island, a heightened understanding of the Bay will, hopefully, result. "CBF starts up in March," she said. "I cook in my home and staff from CBF comes over and takes the food back for the students. I'll cook for twenty-five to thirty students each week. The thing they like best is my mashed potatoes. I peel every one of them. The kids are mostly from the city and have never eaten anything but instant potatoes. They just love my mashed potatoes. I feed them well. I'll offer them a choice of a meat or seafood, a vegetable, corn pudding, rolls, and a two-layered cake. I've cooked for CBF for twenty-eight years."

Mary Ada was once requested to travel to another Chesapeake Bay Foundation outpost on Fox's Island, south of Smith Island, in Virginia. "I agreed to go; Dwight took me down there," she said. "A group of high-ranking officials had kayaked over to the island and I was to cook for them over the weekend. This one gentleman in the group kept hanging around the kitchen. He was drinking coffee as I was packing up to leave on Sunday. He told me he really liked my crab cakes, they were the best he'd ever eaten. During our conversation, I asked him who he worked for. He answered, 'The President.' 'The President of what?' I asked. 'The President of the United States,' he answered. You could've knocked me over with a feather. His name was Chris Burnham. (Burnham was the Under Secretary of State for Management for Condoleezza Rice. He'd also been Assistant Secretary of State for Resource Management and the CFO for former Secretary of State Colin Powell.) He told me that he wanted me to come to Washington for a personal tour of the White House at Christmas time. He also told me that if I had any extra cakes, I could bring one along.

"Author Tom Horton had a home in Tylerton at the time, so Dwight and I and Tom and his wife went to Washington. When we met Chris, I told him I had a gift for him. 'I brought you this book and I also brought the author who wrote it,' I said. He thought that was the neatest thing there ever was. Not only did we tour his massive offices on Capitol Hill, we went through the White House with VIP passes and a personal guide. That was some experience."

It is not all work and no play for Mary Ada Marshall. Every spring she and a group of friends attend "Ladies' Night" on Fox's Island. "About ten or fifteen of my friends

Tylerton store. *Photo by author.*

and I go over to Fox's before our summer work begins," she said. "We stay in the lodge that is owned by the CBF. There are twenty or more beds in the lodge. It is primitive, but there is a generator that provides us with electricity. The boat captain that works for CBF takes us over there and he grills steaks for us. We bring all the other food. We eat and tell stories and come home the next day. We sit around and tell each other yarns. Other than the boat captain, no men are allowed. Last year we went out in a skiff while we were there and a whole school of dolphins swam around the boat. There were twenty of them and they followed our boat for a long time. They were beautiful. It was one of those mornings when it was slick ca'am, not a ripple on the water. The sun was just coming up and it was gorgeous. That was a fun time."

Living on Smith Island requires a high degree of organization. "We have to be organized," said Mary Ada. "You have to be a good manager, too. The men make the money, but the women organize and run the household. That's not always an easy job."

Life on Smith Island continues to be satisfying for Mary Ada. "The best thing about living on this island is sharing," she said. "There's a lot of love here, we're all like one great big family. There is nothing I could ask for that my neighbors wouldn't get for me. Everybody knows everybody, there are no strangers here. We look out for each other. When your neighbors hurt, you hurt with them. I don't want to live anywhere else; I want to stay here just as long as I'm able."

Tylerton sunset. *Photo by author*.

Chapter Six

Mary Parks Harding

A major center for oyster production until the mid-twentieth century, fortunes were made and lost from the bounty that lay beneath the waters surrounding Dorchester County, on Maryland's Eastern Shore. From the Choptank in the north to the Honga in the south, Dorchester rivers were richly endowed with the succulent bivalve.

Hundreds of men toiled on the rivers and bays, harvesting oysters and later crabs. To capture these delicacies, a large fleet of skipjacks and workboats transported their owners to the harvesting grounds. These wooden vessels were, for the most part, constructed on the banks of rivers and creeks so abundantly spread across the county.

Until the late 1950s, one of the more prominent Dorchester boat builders was Bronza Parks of Wingate. About twenty-five miles from Cambridge, in the southern portion of the county, Wingate was home to approximately one hundred people.

"When I was growing up in Wingate, there were eighteen or twenty houses there," said 86-year-old Mary Parks Harding, daughter of Bronza Parks. "Everybody had lived in the community for a long time. Originally, many had migrated there from Holland's Island in the middle of the Bay. The community was very close, everybody knew everybody.

"I remember the roads were made from trees that had been laid down and then filled in with oyster shells. Except for a stretch of about a mile, the road to Cambridge was like that. It was a distance of twenty-five miles. The road wasn't paved until you got to the town of Church Creek, about five miles south of Cambridge."

Very few cars were in Wingate in those days, according to Mary. "Albert Kirwan had a bus and he'd transport groups of people from the southern part of the county to Cambridge, but we didn't need to go to Cambridge very often. Mr. Bob Pritchett had a general store nearby and he sold everything we needed: groceries, dry goods, even chains and ropes for boats. Over in Bishop's Head, Mr. Fred Ruark's store catered to the dredge boat fleet. He had all the supplies they would need, in addition to groceries. Bishop's Head was about six miles from Wingate."

Mary and twin in a baby carriage. *Courtesy of Mary Parks Harding.*

During the warm months, most Wingate households supported large gardens. Vegetables were canned and preserved for use throughout the year. Men provided meat for their tables by hunting ducks and other wildlife so abundant in the area. Cattle and hogs were raised by some households, as were chickens. Seafood was plentiful.

Born in 1927, Mary Parks Harding and her twin sister were the third and fourth of five girls born to Bronza and his wife, Katie. Lucille was the oldest sibling, followed by Irene, the twins, and, finally, Joyce, the youngest. "My father had wanted a boy," Mary laughed. "When my twin sister Martha and I came along, he told us that we had disappointed him twice."

The two older sisters smothered their younger siblings with attention. "Irene was my protector and Lucille was Martha's protector," Mary continued. "One of my earliest memories was being pushed around in a doll baby carriage by my older sisters. Irene still considered me to be hers until she died."

Bronza and Katie lived in a rented home until their two oldest daughters were born. He built a three-room house on land that his grandfather had owned. In later years, additions would be added twice to accommodate the growing family. "Our house was on a fairly high piece of land," Mary explained. "We weren't inconvenienced by high tides like most of the families around us were. Homes in those days were situated to

Parks Family home, Wingate, Maryland.
Courtesy of Mary Parks Harding.

take advantage of cross ventilation. Doors and windows were opposite each other to allow the breezes to circulate."

Void of indoor plumbing, the bathroom was an outhouse, some distance from the main house. Central heat was not available, nor was electricity. Homes were illuminated by kerosene lamps. Food was prepared on a stove fueled by wood. "In the summer, that cook stove made the house unbearably hotter than it usually was," said Mary.

Bronza began his boat-building career before Mary was born. "In 1918, when daddy was only nineteen years old, he and mother's brother went into the seafood processing business," she said. "That was short-lived and by 1920 the factory was closed. That's when daddy started building boats. For years, when a customer wanted a boat built, daddy would go to the customer's home and build the boat in his yard. One of the first dovetailed boats that daddy built was named *Dorothy*. The *Dorothy* was built in Bishop's Head, at the home of Mr. Woodland."

Dovetailed boats are of a distinctive design. Very narrow for their length, dovetails have a reverse sloping stern that adds additional length to the boat. The increased length, along with the narrowness of beam, it was believed, made the design faster than traditionally designed boats. This was important because, in those days, the first boats to arrive at the processing house with their oysters commanded higher prices than those arriving later when the processor had enough oysters needed for the day and prices were cut.

By 1932 or '33, with the Depression behind him, conditions improved and Bronza began building boats adjacent to his own house in Wingate. One of the early boats to come away from the Parks' yard was named the *Martha*. Named for the owner's daughter,

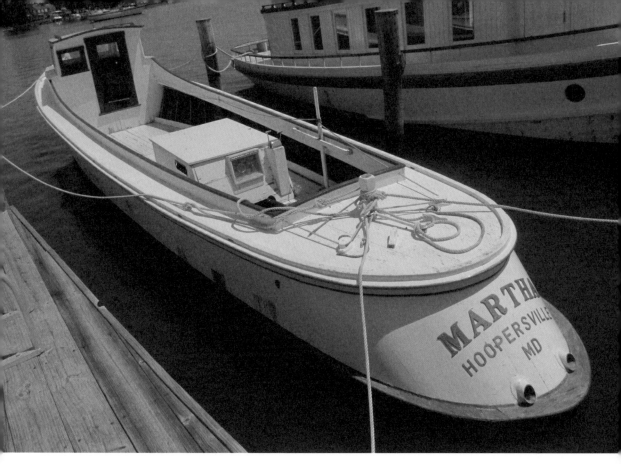

The *Martha* (note the dovetailed stern). *Photo by author.*

she was completed in 1934. At forty-three feet in length and with only an eight-foot beam, the *Martha* was a dovetailed design. Still afloat, the *Martha* is now owned by the Chesapeake Bay Maritime Museum in St. Michaels, Maryland, where she is on display.

Bronza Parks was a large man. "Over six feet tall, barrel chested, with broad shoulders and narrow of hip, he was strong," said Mary. "This came in handy in those days because there was no mechanization. Everything was done with hand tools. Later, one of his first power tools was a band saw powered by a gasoline engine."

Mary and her sisters attended a one-room school, about three-quarters-of-a-mile from their home. "When the roads were icy, mother would walk with us through a neighbor's woods. The route was longer, but it was safer than being on the road," said Mary. "We seldom missed school. Most of the kids in Wingate had perfect attendance every year. I still have one of my perfect attendance certificates."

Seldom did weather hinder school attendance. "One time the tide was extremely high and we couldn't get through it to get to school," Mary recalled. "My mother put us all in a skiff and pushed us through the tide to school. That's the way things were in those days."

There were seven grades in the one-room school that the Parks girls attended. Staffed by one teacher, there were tables placed throughout the room. When it was time to work with a specific grade level, the teacher would have the students who were in that grade come to the front table and she would work with them as a group while other students studied quietly at their tables. "Miss Jenny Jones was our teacher," Mary went on. "There were only twenty-five or thirty-five kids in the entire school."

Mary's mother would awaken very early to prepare her children's lunch. Often she'd fry pork chops or make soup for them to take to school. She would place the food in a glass jar, which would be placed in a large pot of heated water on the stove at school. In that way, lunch would be warmed. "I'd look at kids that had store-bought bread or meat to go on sandwiches and think how lucky they were," recounted Mary. "My mother even had to make the biscuits we brought to school."

During the depths of the Depression, Mary recalled watching cars pull into houses delivering food. "I thought those people must have been rich or something," she said. "I wondered why we couldn't get some of the food like my neighbors were getting. Later I found out that the deliveries were coming from the Welfare Department."

Mary explained that there were always things to do for entertainment. Ice skating was a favorite activity in the winter. "Mom and dad were beautiful skaters," she said. "In the summer, we played outside. Seldom did we go in the house. Boys played ball in the yard and the men played ball on weekends. Men also enjoyed pitching horseshoes. As things got better, we got a radio and at night we'd listen to the broadcasts. The radio had an antenna attached to it. It was real high, on a pole, and sometimes, when the wind blew hard, the antenna would be bent over from the wind."

Every night after dinner Mary and her sisters would go outside, sit on the steps, and gaze at the sky. "We identified constellations in the sky," she said. "We also could look at a leaf and identify the type of tree it came from. We'd listen to birds sing. We enjoyed nature."

When Mary was in the sixth grade, a new student moved into the area and attended the school. "He was in my same grade," she explained. "I used to hang around with the boys. I liked to play ball and do the things that boys did. My sisters were prissy and feminine, but not me. Anyway, this boy got so he'd chase me around, telling me he was going to kiss me. I didn't like that, so I told my cousin, Willis McGlaughlin, who was the biggest boy in school. He told me to stand near him wherever he went and nothing would happen to me. He was playing ball and I was close by. He swung at a ball and the bat came around and struck me in the face. It broke my nose and cheek bone. Mom and dad took me to the doctor and he told them to keep me home from school the next day (Friday), but I'd be OK to return on Monday. When I got home from visiting the doctor, I lapsed into unconsciousness for three days. I was really sick. The preacher visited and my father told him, 'Little Mary is not really doing that good.' I heard dad tell the preacher that and I yelled for mom. That's when I woke up. They all came running into the room. I missed about two months of school recovering from that injury."

Following grade seven, Mary attended high school in the town of Crapo, which was six miles from Wingate. "We rode a bus to high school," said Mary. "We'd walk a half-mile to the place where we'd meet the bus. It took over an hour to get to school because the bus went all over that section of the county picking up kids."

High School was a three-room affair. Three teachers staffed the school. One teacher concentrated on science, another math, and the third, Latin and grammar. Students would rotate among the rooms at the sound of a bell. "I studied Latin for four years," Mary said. "I enjoyed school very much. After grade 11, we graduated."

As a teenager, Mary, like many women and girls in the southern portion of Dorchester County, worked in a seafood processing facility during summers. "There were two seafood processing plants in Wingate in those days," said Mary. "Local women worked in those factories separating the meat from the crab's shell (picking). Crabs were cooked in large steamers. I can still remember the sweet aroma that drifted through our community as crabs were being steamed.

"There were no age limits for working in the factories in those days, so, during summer, when school was not in session, kids worked in the factories cracking claws. A loud whistle would sound to let the workers in the community know when work was available. I helped process crabs by cracking claws at George Robinson's facility in Wingate. In the beginning, I made two cents for each pound of claw meat I picked. The crabs were always fat. Later, I earned five cents a pound. Some weeks I made $9, a lot of money back then. The women who picked crabs were paid ten cents per pound.

"The factory was like a meeting place for women to socialize and share neighborhood news. Sometimes, they would even sing as they worked. It was a pleasant place to work and I really enjoyed the experience."

One day, when Lucille was in high school, she came home and said that a man had visited the school from Salisbury State Teacher's College. His name was Dr. Blackwell. She explained that he was searching for future students. Bronza asked his daughter, "You told him you'd go, didn't you?" Lucille replied in the negative and her father told her to get word to him that she'd be interested in attending. Lucille enrolled at Salisbury and later began a teaching career that spanned several decades. "All her life she was a teacher," said Mary.

World War II had a profound effect on the family. "I remember vividly the day that our neighbor, Miss Mildred, yelled over and told my mother that Pearl Harbor had been bombed by the Japanese," Mary said. "That was devastating news. One of our boys, Johnny Thomas, was in Normandy and he didn't come home. It was so sad! But everybody realized that it was necessary that we were in the war. That's the way it was back then. We had a lot of faith in our leaders."

During World War I, Mary's father had received a draft notice. "He never had to serve though," said Mary. "But his brother, Orville, was drafted and sent overseas. He was in combat, but he came home unharmed."

Following graduation from high school in 1944, Mary and her twin sister attended business school at Goldey Business College in Wilmington, Delaware. "We lived together in Wilmington," Mary stated. "We'd take a train in Cambridge to get to Wilmington. It was a freight train, but it had one passenger car attached. If there were more passengers than seats, we had to sit on boxes in the freight cars. The trip was very long. The train would stop at every little town along the way. It took a long time to get to Wilmington."

Finishing business school in 1946, Mary returned home. "I got a job in Cambridge at the Phillips Packing Company," Mary stated.

Through the years, Bronza's boat-building operation flourished. He built a fifty-foot building near his home in which he built boats. In this manner, he wasn't hampered by inclement weather. As additional orders for boats came in, the shop was expanded twice more. Eventually, the boat-building operation would be housed in a 150-foot building, allowing him to build up to five boats at a time inside the building. Boats were constructed upside down. After the bottom, stern and sides were attached; the boat was then turned upright and taken out into the yard, where it was finished.

"There were always kids around who played in our yard," Mary said. "We enjoyed going into the boathouse and playing in the shavings. The men kept an eye on us, but they never said we shouldn't be in there.

"In the late 1930s dad bought his own electrical plant," said Mary. In the back of one of the buildings there was a section where over twenty batteries were encased in glass. They were lined up like stair steps. The batteries provided thirty-two volts, enough to provide power for his tools.

"Daddy got a man to come down and run wires from the boat-building plant to the house. That way we could have electricity in our home as well. Mother could then have

Boat-building shed. *Courtesy Mary Parks Harding.*

an electric iron. Before that, she used an iron heated by gasoline. There was a circular tank on the iron that held the gasoline. On the bottom of the tank were small holes that, when lit, heated the iron's surface. We still had that iron until a few years ago; I don't know whatever happened to it."

About that time, telephone service was extended to Wingate. "Our phone hung on the wall," stated Mary. "You had to crank it to dial a number. Our number was 3F32. That meant to call our house required three long cranks and two short ones. The number over in the boat shop was 9F32. When our phone rang, everybody along the line picked up to listen in on the conversation. They wanted to know what was going on. People didn't really mind. Everybody shared with everybody else.

"The telephone operator was up in Golden Hill. You didn't ever try to make a call after 9 p.m. unless it was an emergency. Usually emergencies meant that there was a death. Sickness back then was not considered an emergency. Because ours was one of only six phones in Wingate, we sometimes got calls for our neighbors telling of a death in the family. When that happened, daddy would have to go to the neighbor's house to deliver the bad news.

"Deaths back then were treated differently than today. When a death occurred in the community, there was very little activity until the deceased was buried. Clothes were not hung out on the lines and grass was not cut. This was out of respect.

"Bodies were laid out in the home of the deceased, usually in the parlor. Many were buried in family gravesites adjacent to the house. Funeral services were held in the home of the person who had died. Later, bodies were taken to the church for the funeral and burial took place there. The first hearse I ever saw looked like an elongated Model T Ford. It had a truck body that had black curtains in all the windows."

Eventually, telephone service improved and dial service was installed. "My father made the very first phone call from Wingate after we got dial service," said Mary. "He called the mayor of Cambridge."

As the years advanced, Bronza's business increased dramatically. By the 1940s, he was enjoying the reputation as one of the most proficient boat-builders in the area. Customers came from far away for a Parks-built vessel. Bronza built only boats that had been ordered. No boats were built on speculation. Ultimately, over four hundred boats would come from his shop in Wingate. From fourteen-foot skiffs to sixty-foot cabin cruisers and, eventually, skipjacks, Bronza was a master builder.

In the early days, after boats were built, they traveled toward the water over rollers made from gum trees and pulled by a team of oxen. Wingate harbor, where the boats were launched, was about a quarter-mile from the shop. Walking behind the boat as it headed toward the launch site, Bronza used a plank in such a manner that he could turn the boat as needed as it proceeded down the

Wingate Harbor. *Courtesy of Mary Parks Harding.*

Mary on the *WILMA LEE*, with Ralph Ruark at the helm.
Courtesy of Mary Parks Harding.

road. Later, he used a truck for that operation. Boats were launched at high tide. Logs were placed in parallel, running down into the water and heavily greased. The boat was positioned atop the logs and slid down into the water. Launching was labor intensive. "Dad bought a siren and mounted it on top of one of the buildings," said Mary. "When the time was right for launching a boat, dad would sound the siren and the men of the community would come to help with the launching."

The first skipjack Bronza built was the *Wilma Lee*. The boat was forty-seven feet in length with a beam of sixteen feet. With a draft of four and a half feet, the vessel weighed twenty tons. She was built for Mary's uncle, Asbury. Bronza constructed the boat in 1940. After Asbury's death, Mary's brother-in-law, Captain Ralph Ruark, bought the boat. "I used to go on the boat every year when it went to the annual skipjack races at Deal Island," said Mary. "That was always a lot of fun. We always did well in the races. Capt. Ruark was a good captain. The boat is presently in Ocracoke, North Carolina." When the *Wilma Lee* was built, there were no less than fifteen boats under construction in the Parks boat yard.

Perhaps the most famous skipjack to come out of Bronza's yard was the *Rosie Parks*. Three skipjacks were built at the same time. In addition to the *Rosie*, the *Martha Lewis* and *Lady Katie* were built simultaneously. Finished in 1955, the three vessels had identical dimensions. They were forty-six feet in length with an eighteen-foot beam and a draft slightly over three feet. The *Rosie Parks* was built for Orville, and James Lewis contracted for the *Martha Lewis*. Prior to the launching of the *Lady Katie*, the owner had a heart attack and died.

"Dad said he had built a lot of boats for other people, but had never kept one for himself," said Mary. "He said he was going to keep the third skipjack. Before he named it, I tried to get him to name the boat after me, but he said, 'No, I'm going to name her after my best girl.' The boat was named for my mother." The *Lady Katie* is currently privately owned and continues to dredge for oysters.

The *Rosie Parks* went on to have a stellar career on the oyster bars of Maryland. Orville Parks would become one of the most respected skipjack captains in the Chesapeake. He was also a perpetual winner of skipjack races, both at Deal Island and Sandy Point. As a result, the *Rosie*, with Orville at the helm, was arguably the best-known skipjack in the Bay. Before ending his career, Governor J. Millard Tawes honored Orville by appointing him Admiral of the Chesapeake. The *Rosie Parks* is presently owned by the Chesapeake Bay Maritime Museum in St. Michaels, Maryland. She recently underwent a complete restoration and will again proudly sail the waters of the Chesapeake.

After her oystering days ended, the *Martha Lewis* was relocated to the northern Chesapeake. She is owned and operated by an organization in Havre de Grace and used for ecotourism.

Bronza was a gracious and generous host. Often, when customers visited his shop, he'd invite them into his house for a luncheon of crab cakes or other seafood treats. He counted among his close friends Maryland Governors J. Millard Tawes and William Preston Lane. "He treated everybody the same, whether you were rich or poor," said Mary. "One time he and another man were in Cambridge working on a boat. At lunchtime, they went into a local restaurant. Daddy sat down and ordered, and the owner whispered to him that he couldn't serve his companion who was black. Daddy looked at him and said, 'Just cancel my order then, we'll find another place to eat.' To dad, race was not an issue. He respected everybody. He never felt he was better than anyone else."

A community leader as well as a business leader, Bronza was the driving force behind the formation of the Lakes and Straits Volunteer Fire Co. and later served as its President. "A man was working under a house over in Crapo and he touched a live wire and was electrocuted," Mary said. "That bothered daddy a lot. He said that if we

The *Rosie Parks* in final stages of restoration. *Photo by author.*

had only had an ambulance in the community the man might have survived. Later, he went door-to-door, getting pledges to buy an ambulance. A year and a half after getting the ambulance, a fire hall was built in the community." Today, the Lakes and Straits Volunteer Fire Co. sits on the land where Bronza's boat shop was originally located.

The Phillips Packing Company of Cambridge, where Mary worked, was an enormous food-processing business. The majority of the southern portion of the town was covered with gigantic buildings belonging to the Phillips Company. At its height, Phillips employed over 6,000 people. So massive was the business that it published its own newspaper. A modern baseball stadium was built for employee use, and future Hall of Famers played on Phillips field. Among them was Jimmy Foxx, who hailed from the Eastern Shore town of Sudlersville. Phillips was the largest cannery on the East Coast and one of the largest in the country. "Lots of food was processed there for the war effort," said Mary. "In addition to seafood, vegetables were processed for canning under the brand name 'Phillips Delicious.'"

Mary worked in the main office of the company, which covered the second floor of the Phillps Hardware Store in downtown Cambridge. "I rented a room in Cambridge on Belvedere Avenue," she said. "My landlady rented mostly to teachers who worked in county schools, but I was lucky enough to live there during my tenure at Phillips. I was an auditor in the billing department. There was a huge computer located along the back wall in our office that was used by the company. The computer was enormous and covered quite a bit of floor space. By that time, I was married and, during my time with Phillips, had gotten pregnant. At the time, it was a practice not to employ women after their fourth month of pregnancy, so I had to leave Phillips.

"After the birth of my daughter (Brenda Goodwin) and son (Warren 'Pres' Harding), I returned to work. I was always fascinated with the phone company. I went to work in the telephone office in Cambridge and loved every minute of it. For nine years, I worked at the Cambridge office and worked myself up to chief evening operator. I made $28 weekly when I started and thought that was all the money in the world."

Transfers took Mary to Havre de Grace, Chestertown, Salisbury, and Glen Burnie. She was later appointed Financial Manager for AT&T Operator Services in Maryland and central Pennsylvania. In 1988, she retired and returned to Cambridge the following year to live.

On May 13, 1958, Mary was working a split shift (10-1 and 5-9) at the telephone company when she received a call from her dad. He explained that he was coming to Cambridge and invited Mary to have lunch with him. After lunch, the pair went to the office of the state's attorney, C. Burnam Mace, who had prepared a lien against Willis C. Rowe, for whom Bronza was building an eighteen-foot skipjack. A veteran of World War II and a law school graduate, Willis C. Rowe lived in Silver Spring, Maryland. "Daddy asked Mr. Mace to delay serving the papers because Rowe was coming that afternoon and he felt sure that everything could be worked out," said Mary. "He further explained that he had told Rowe that he was welcome to bring any reputable boat-builder with him when he visited in order to get a second opinion regarding the cost of the project."

Later, after returning to work, Mary received a frantic phone call from her mother. "It was a few minutes after 5," she said. "I could hardly understand what she was saying. She told me that Rowe had shot and killed daddy. I called my husband and we rushed down to Wingate."

James Richardson, a well-respected boat-builder from near Cambridge, had accompanied Rowe to Bronza's boat yard. "He later told me that he had told Rowe the price of the boat being built by dad was fair. He further told Rowe that had he been building the boat the price would have been higher.

"Rowe went into the boat shop while Richardson remained in the car. Richardson heard a noise that sounded like a flat board smacking against another. Two more bangs rang out immediately after the first. He ran into the building and found dad dead and Rowe nearby holding a 38-caliber handgun."

At age fifty-nine, Bronza Parks was dead; 39-year-old Willis C. Rowe was subsequently sentenced to eighteen years in prison for second-degree murder. Katie and her daughters attended the trial each day. Daily, they dressed in black.

The funeral was held in Cambridge at Grace Methodist Church. The large sanctuary was filled to capacity and mourners stood outside. Flowers lined the entire interior of the church and flowed upstairs into the choir loft.

Years earlier, after purchasing their cemetery plots, Katie asked Bronza how he felt about selecting a tombstone. He replied that he'd rather be remembered for the manner in which he lived his life and didn't feel a need for a memorial. "I don't think he'll ever be forgotten," stated Mary.

That fateful day in May ended the illustrious career of one of the Chesapeake's finest craftsmen. Among other places, his legacy lives on at the Chesapeake Bay Maritime Museum, where the *Rosie Parks* serves as an appropriate memorial to her builder.

"Our family was never the same after that day," Mary said. "It was very hard for all of us. My mother would sit in dad's rocking chair for hours on end. She was distraught. We never recovered from dad's death."

Mary and her sister, Joyce, flanking the life-size image of
Bronza Parks at Chesapeake Bay Maritime Museum.
Courtesy of Mary Parks Harding.

CHAPTER SEVEN

Captain Iris Clarke

On a chilly late September afternoon, Captain Iris Clarke turned the key and the diesel engine in her 41-foot sailboat roared to life. The sun was settling lower in the sky as the *Selina II* gently eased away from her berth in the St. Michaels, Maryland harbor on the Eastern Shore. Two guests from Virginia were aboard for the sunset cruise. They relaxed in comfortable director's chairs as Captain Iris slowly maneuvered the boat through the crowded harbor, pointing out interesting landmarks. "The *Selina II* was built in 1926," she announced. "My grandfather had her built and she has been part of our family for six generations."

Captain Iris' life is intertwined with the *Selina II*. She grew up with the boat. Sanding, varnishing, maintaining the boat, and sailing her have been a large part of Iris' life for as long as she can remember. The boat has been passed down through her maternal side of the family for generations. "My family is interesting," she said. "It's a rags to riches story."

Iris' great-grandfather, Samuel Hird, emigrated to the United States in the late 1800s. At the age of twenty-one, he sailed from his native England, where he had been an itinerant mill worker. Also on the ship was seventeen-year-old Selina, who would later become his wife. Arriving in this country, he continued to work in woolen mills up and down the East Coast wherever he could find work. Eventually, he entered into a partnership with a fellow mill worker and the pair parlayed enough money to buy a mill in Ridgewood, New Jersey. After a couple of years, the partnership was dissolved, but Samuel stayed on at the mill.

Following the Civil War, fabrics were lot-dyed. Primarily, fabrics were either blue, black, or brown. There was little variation in color. People desired more colorful fabric for clothing. Samuel found that instead of taking woven fabric and dyeing it as a lot, he could weave different colored threads together to make different colored fabric, as well as a variety of patterns. His mill was very successful and he sold a tremendous amount of fabric. He made a small fortune.

The SELINA II. Photo by author.

Samuel and his family vacationed in a well-to-do community at the end of Long Island, named Shelter Island. He built a vacation home in Dering Harbor, where the family lived quite comfortably. Lavishly appointed, an elevator was installed in the home and an entourage accompanied the family during their summers on Long Island, including a gardener, cook, butler, and chauffeur. Eventually, Samuel passed his fortune, his home, and his business to his son, Ainsworth.

Ainsworth continued running the mill in New Jersey and, for a time, business was brisk. Ainsworth was responsible for having the *Selina II* built. She was his second boat;

Selina I had been a long, narrow, open powerboat that was unstable. Ainsworth and his family were aboard the *Selina I* for an outing one day. In addition to his wife Mildred, their nine-year-old daughter, six-year-old son, and an infant daughter were aboard. The family ventured out to the east end of Long Island, to a place called Plum Gut, a narrow channel that could become uncomfortable when the wind and tide ran in opposite directions. As the boat turned to head for home, the unstable craft rolled violently and the boat shipped water. Mildred was terrified and her husband dutifully abandoned the vessel thereafter.

About a year later, Ainsworth and Mildred were invited for a sail on a friend's catboat. With a beam (width) half as wide as the boat's length, catboats are very stable. Mildred was impressed and gave Ainsworth the approval to build another boat, as long as it was a catboat. Ainsworth visited the H. W. Sweet Shipyard in Greenport, New York, pointed to a Crosby-designed catboat, and told the builder to build him one, "Just like that one, only bigger."

Not wanting to pass up a contract, the builder said that he had only built powerboats in the past, never a sailboat. He further explained that he didn't know how to build a centerboard (to keep the boat tracking on a more or less straight line while under sail) or the trunk into which it rested. Ainsworth told him to build the boat without a centerboard, as he had no intention of sailing the boat; his intended use was for fishing and the boat would be operated by a hired captain.

"So the boat was built without a centerboard," stated Iris. "That's partially the reason the boat has survived these many years. Centerboards are prone to leakage and rot. Another reason she has survived is because she was built of longleaf Georgia pine. Georgia pine is known to be fairly rot-resistant. She was also built to yacht standards rather than workboat standards."

In 1929, the stock market crashed and the country entered in to the Great Depression. Like many others, Ainsworth's business suffered. Sensing that the country was on the brink of involvement in World War II, Ainsworth attempted to hold on. He knew there would, again, be a demand for fabric during the war years. By the time the war broke out, however, the DuPont Company had introduced nylon and polyester. Within a few years, little remained of the family fortune.

Ainsworth sailed *Selina II* until 1962. The boat was passed down to his daughter, Esther, and son-in-law, Bridgford Hunt. Bridgford and Esther would parent three children, two boys and a girl. The girl, whose given name is Selina, would come to be known as Iris. "There were girls named Selina in our family for seven generations," said Iris. "In high school, I was nicknamed Iris and I've been known as Iris ever since."

Bridgford and Esther made their home in Montclair, New Jersey, and Bridgford commuted daily to New York City, where he worked in a management consulting firm. Weekends and holidays were spent on Shelter Island.

Selina II was under Bridgford and Esther's care for the next thirty-nine years. "He passed the boat down to me in 2001," said Iris. "My oldest brother had done a lot of work on the boat in the 1980s and all that effort satisfied his boating interest. He had no problem with my getting the *Selina II*. My other brother wasn't very good with his hands and knew that owning the boat was not what he wanted, so I ended up with her. The *Selina II* has a beam over twenty feet. Not only is she quite stable, she also has a tremendous cargo capacity. She is capable of carrying 40,000 pounds."

Catboats were developed in the nineteenth century in New Jersey and Massachusetts. By 1850, there were lots of them and they were used as passenger ferries and miniature freighters because of their holding capacity. In New England, they were prevalent in the commercial fishing industry, again because of their stability and cargo capacity. The *Selina II* is the largest surviving catboat in the country; only five catboats were ever built over forty feet in length.

The *Selina I*. *Courtesy of Captain Iris Clarke*.

Catboats are propelled by a single sail, the mast of which is mounted further forward than on most sailboats. The sail area is much larger than on other designs. The *Selina II's* sail area is almost 1,000 square feet and rests on a boom that is thirty-five feet long and weighs six hundred pounds.

By the time Iris took over the *Selina II*, she had finished college and done graduate work in computers at New York University. In 1981, she married and, in 1982, relocated to Somerset County, south of Salisbury, Maryland. She and her husband, an artist named C. D. Clarke, were married for twenty-five years before agreeing to divorce.

"When I finished college, I had two desires," she said. "First, I wanted to live on the water; and secondly, I wanted a career in computer sciences. We looked around for an affordable place on the water. North of New York, waterfront property is very expensive, so that was out. We started looking to the south. We weren't thrilled with New Jersey and all the nuclear plants and Delaware was also not very appealing. We drove down to Maryland and looked around. We found a derelict house in Frenchtown, south of Salisbury, in Somerset County. The house sat on slightly more than two waterfront acres. We paid $20,000 for the place and moved down.

"Initially, I found a job working with computers at a local steel company; later, I was Vice President of Operations for a software firm. Eventually, I ended up doing marketing for my husband, who, by then, had become quite successful as an artist."

Concerned with the expense of upkeep for the boat, Iris decided to have the boat pay her own way. She earned her captain's license and readied to sail the *Selina II* to the Chesapeake for a life of chartering. "When I told my mother about my plans to bring the boat south, she objected," said Iris. "Mother wanted me to wait a year so the boat could celebrate her seventy-fifth birthday on Shelter Island, so I waited a year before bringing her down.

"Mother threw a big party for the *Selina II* in July 2001. There were 350 people who came to the open house, or open boat. Food and drinks were abundant and everyone had a good time. The party was held on a Saturday. The following Monday, we headed south in the boat."

The trip south was eventful. In addition to her husband, Iris' dad was on the boat, along with other friends. Long Island Sound was overcast and cloudy. As they passed the twin towers of the World Trade Center in New York City, rain clouds obscured the buildings in such a way that they looked exactly like they did after the disaster of 9-11. "It was uncanny," Iris stated.

The weather was miserable and the boat was weathered in at Sandy Hook for three days. Escorted by heavy seas and strong winds, they surfed into Atlantic City, where they remained overnight. In Cape May, they stayed for an additional three days. "My father was really itchy to get away from Cape May," Iris said. "I was leery about leaving because Delaware Bay can really be nasty and there is no shelter to duck into, but, because of my dad, we left and entered Delaware Bay. A short time later, the waves began to build and spray was being thrown all over the boat. I asked if anybody wanted to turn back. No one responded. The boat, however, began making noises like I had never heard before. I said, 'Well, someone here is willing to answer my question,' and I turned the wheel and headed back to Cape May for a couple more days."

Eventually, Iris and crew were able to cross Delaware Bay, enter the C and D Canal, and head south for St. Michaels. In St. Michaels, they moored at the Chesapeake Bay Maritime Museum. The staff was very helpful and asked if anything was needed. Realizing the boat was leaking badly, it was recommended that she contact Mike Vlahovich, a wooden boat expert, to identify needed repairs. Iris sailed the boat to Cambridge, where the boat was hauled out for inspection.

"Mike handed me a two-page list of things that needed repair," said Iris. "Had I known then what I know now, I might have scuttled her on the spot. I took the list to five different boat yards and got estimates ranging from $8,000 to $76,000. All were way under the eventual repair bill."

The boat was taken to James Richardson's yard south of Cambridge and Tom Howell spent nine months working on the boat. Major repairs were made and, when back in the water, the boat remained in Cambridge for the rest of the abbreviated sailing season.

The following year, Iris worked out of Tilghman Island in Talbot County. She moored the boat alongside a waterfront restaurant, distributed brochures, and spread the word that the *Selina II* was available for chartering.

Desiring to be located in tourist-rich St. Michaels, Iris visited the town, searching for a place to moor the boat. Meeting the dock master at the Harbor Inn Hotel and Marina, she was informed that the sailing vessel that had previously operated from their marina would not be returning. Iris arranged to relocate her business there for the 2004 season.

Living on the boat for the first five years, she sailed out of St. Michaels. Iris was less than pleased. "It was not the greatest lifestyle," she said. "I had to use public showers at the marina and sleep in a cabin that sometimes reached a hundred degrees. Constantly eating unhealthy restaurant food was also a turnoff."

Iris and her father (age 89). *Courtesy of Captain Iris Clarke.*

Iris began investigating the possibility of renting a home in the St. Michaels area. Instead of renting, she found a rundown house that was for sale. After demolishing the house, she had a new home built and took occupancy in 2006. Presently, she lives in the house during sailing season.

The well-muscled young mate hoisted the sail on the *Selina II* as the boat entered the Miles River. Puffy, cotton ball clouds hovered low off the water and cast their shadows on the river. Likewise, the sun was magnificently brilliant as it reflected off the water. The Virginia couple donned light jackets to ward off the evening chill. A light breeze filled the sail and the *Selina II* came to life.

Captain Iris will host approximately 1,000 passengers on the *Selina II* annually. She estimates that 12,000 passengers have cruised on the boat since she's owned her.

Iris Clarke works hard for the money she earns. In season, she is on the boat seven days a week. Her day begins at 8 a.m. and many times doesn't end until 10:30 or 11 p.m. "It can be a long day," she said. "But I enjoy being out here on the boat and interacting with the folks who visit the town." She estimates that her work week exceeds sixty hours.

The *Selina II* makes four trips each day. Two-hour trips are scheduled at 10 a.m., 12:30 p.m., and 3 p.m. At 5:30, a champagne sunset cruise takes place. "Sometimes in the summer, when the days are longer, I'll schedule another cruise from 7:30 until 9:30," she explained. "By the time we're finished for the day, I have no difficulty sleeping."

In addition to the daily cruise schedule, Captain Iris offers overnight trips. The *Selina II* can accommodate six passengers for overnights. There are three double berths in the cabin below deck, where passengers sleep family-style. Sleeping on deck is also an option. "We don't do many overnights," she said. "When we do, we leave at 5:30 and return by mid-morning the next day. We provide dinner on the boat and a quiche breakfast the next morning."

On a cabin wall is a bell that is original to the boat. The bell's rope was tied by a master knotsman and includes five knots for good luck. Interwoven inside the rope is a paper with a Psalm inscribed on it. This insures that if the boat were to go down, the crew would be blessed by these Biblical words.

Iris also performs about ten weddings each season on the boat. "I got myself ordained the modern way," she smiled. "I did it on the internet. I'm affiliated with Universal Ministries. I could have gone the Justice of the Peace route, but I feel there is a spiritual base for marriage. It's truly an honor to be a part of a couple's wedding ceremony. Each marriage I perform is tailored for the couple and I try to make the occasion very special. This coming season I'll perform my 100th wedding ceremony." Since the *Selina II* only sails with six passengers at a time, weddings are intimate affairs.

"I've also been asked to spread ashes from the boat. We don't do it very often, only four times so far. We do a symbolic spreading with a small handful of ashes. We don't want to be guilty of pollution."

Captain Iris at the wheel. *Photo by author.*

Captain Iris in wedding attire.
Courtesy of Captain Iris Clarke.

The *Selina II* has also been the location for a number of photo shoots, not only for magazines, but also a nationwide department store chain did a photo shoot on the boat.

In the distance, a group of sailboats were racing. "Every Wednesday evening, there are sailboat races on the Miles River," Iris explained. "If you'd like, we can get closer to watch the start of the race. That's usually pretty exciting as the boats try to outdo each other to reach the starting line at precisely the correct moment." Getting the nod of approval from the Virginia couple, the *Selina II* headed toward the racing fleet. As they passed, many of the skippers and crew waved and greeted Iris good-naturedly. "Looking good," she said, flashing her trademark smile. "You got a good start today."

After the racing fleet sped by, Capt. Iris spun the wheel and headed upriver. Disappearing into the cabin, she reappeared momentarily with a generous assortment of wines, cheeses, and hors d' oeuvres. After filling drink orders, she discussed the characteristics of her boat. "She has a wonderful heart," she said of the *Selina II*. "She is very lady-like. She never gives me trouble while we're out in the river. The only time she has failed me was when we were at the dock. Her engine failed once, but that was before she left her slip — that's the only time she refused to go sailing for me. She's a great boat."

Convinced that the boat has communicative powers, Iris feels that the *Selina II* lets her know when things aren't as they should be. "Like that time in Delaware Bay, for example," she said. "My dad felt the same way about *Selina II*'s powers.

"On January 1, 2012, he died at the age of ninety. He had been a big fan of Jackie Gleason and the TV show *The Honeymooners*. He passed away while watching a rerun of the show.

"My mother is planning a trip to Spain in the off season next winter. I'm planning to go with her."

An inquiry was made about where the *Selina II* spends the off season. "I used to take her to Virginia for the winter," Iris said in response. "But this year she'll spend the winter in Cambridge. One of the marinas there has a lift large enough to take her out of the water. I'll spend most of the winter refurbishing her, getting her ready for the next sailing season. For example, there are twelve wooden blocks that various lines run through during the course of sailing. I'll take each block apart and lubricate and refinish it before reinstalling it on the boat. I'll spend about four hours working on each of the twelve blocks. *Selina II* requires a lot of maintenance. I try to keep her in tip-top shape."

Celebrities have sailed with Iris. "Actress Jane Seymour and her husband, actor-director James Keach (brother of actor Stacy Keach), sailed on *Selina II*," she said. "They were in town for the filming of the movie, *Wedding Crashers*. A portion of the film was shot here in St. Michaels." The former Mayor of Washington, D. C., Marion Barry, also sailed on the boat, as have professional athletes and sports figures.

"One of the most fascinating and interesting groups to sail on the boat was a group of people who were attending a symposium at the Harbortowne Resort," Iris continued. "The group was made up of medical doctors, engineers, physicists, and other professionals. They were meeting to discuss possibilities for future prosthetic limb development. Their conversations were fascinating, as they talked about the next generation of prosthetic devices being controlled in a similar manner as natural limbs. It's great to see the developments they discussed as possibilities while on *Selina II* become a reality."

Iris explained that she was, at one time, very concerned about what would happen to the boat as she got older. "My brothers have no interest in owning *Selina II*, so I looked to the next generation," she said. "I'd like to see the boat continue to be used in the same way that she is being used today. There are only four great-grandchildren and the oldest happens to be named Selina. She has shown an interest in taking over the boat. Her best friend is a sailor and she will soon marry a professional yacht captain. They have agreed that, when it is time, they'll continue to care for, and run the boat, as I have. I'd hate to see the boat languishing as a museum piece or tied to a dock somewhere unused. She needs to be out sailing and helping folks experience the history of sail.

"I think I solved the financial burden of ownership by taking out a $4,000,000 life insurance policy on myself. My nieces and nephews have been named trustees and the expenses for maintaining the boat will come from the proceeds of the policy. It is comforting to know that *Selina II* will continue sailing for many years after I'm gone."

Following a run towards the headwaters of the Miles River, Capt. Iris again turned the *Selina II* and headed back toward St. Michaels. The brilliant sun was beginning to disappear beneath the horizon, leaving an orange glow on the surface of the river. The mate clamored up to the mast and began lowering the massive sail, signaling an end to a pleasant trip.

Once again docked at the marina, the Virginia couple thanked Captain Iris for a magnificent sail. "I just love sailing on this boat," the female half of the Virginia couple said. "Sailing with Captain Iris is like receiving a thousand hugs. She is a terrific lady!"

Sunset over the *Selina II*'s stern. *Photo by author.*

Chapter Eight

Janet Rippons Ruark

Geographically, Dorchester is the largest county in the state of Maryland. The northern portion is comprised of lands interrupted by gently rolling, albeit very short hills. Rich soils in this area produce an abundance of healthy crops that grace tables for hundreds of miles.

Characteristics differ in the land further south. The gentle relief, so notable in the north, is gradually reduced to flatlands, barely above sea level. Here, the land surrenders to marshes and wetlands. Heavily punctuated by the presence of water, solid ground is often difficult to find. Rivers, creeks, streams, and drainage ditches are everywhere. Cattails bloom, marsh grass is abundant, and creatures seldom seen in other parts of the county roam about freely.

There is a wild beauty here! Nature has painted a fascinating portrait and seen fit to share it with anyone willing to gaze upon her marvelous work. It is a peaceful place, filled with wonderment and magnificence.

On a finger of land splitting away from a southern peninsula lies the settlement of Hoopers Island. About twenty-five miles south of Cambridge, Hoopers is composed of a series of three islands, of which the first two are inhabited and connected to the mainland by high, arcing bridges. The third island has not been inhabited for many years and is accessible only by boat.

To the west of the islands lies the majestic Chesapeake Bay. On the eastern side of the islands is the Honga River. The inhabited islands are referred to as upper and middle Hoopers Island and are home to the communities of Fishing Creek and Hoopersville. Hoopersville, on the middle island, is where Janet Rippons Ruark calls home.

"I've lived here all my life," explained the affable Janet. "My family, on both sides, has lived here for generations. My father's side can be traced back to the 1600s, when the island was settled by a man named Hooper. My mother's family goes back to the colony of Williamsburg. It was from Williamsburg that the first settlers ventured to Maryland and Hoopers Island."

Rippons Seafood. *Photo by author.*

One of Janet's earliest memories is fishing crab floats (separating soft crabs as they undergo the molting process in wooden crate-like cages anchored in the river) with her grandfather, Chandus Rippons, Sr. "I was very young, I guess I came about up to his knee in height," she said. "It was late in the afternoon and my grandfather was fishing up the floats. As he fished out a soft crab, he'd hand it to me to put in a bin. I asked, 'Pop, how do you know which crabs are soft crabs?' He looked down at me and said, 'Janet, when you've fished as many of these as I have, you'll know too.' As a teenager, he had about thirty crab floats that he tended all season."

Chandus Rippons, Sr. came from a large family that had five boys and three girls. His father died in 1927 and a few years later the Depression hit. During the Depression, he stopped working on the water and went to Baltimore for employment. There was easy access to Baltimore back then. A steamboat made regular stops at the island. As soon as he could, he moved back to the island and, once again, worked soft crab floats. This marked the beginning of his involvement in the crab business.

"In 1947, my grandfather and his two brothers, Gene and Irving, along with their uncle, William 'Doc' Rippons, started a crab business," said Janet. "Later that same year, they put up a building and called their business Rippons Bros. Seafood."

The basin that ran from the river to the plant was not deep enough for boats to come in to the plant in order to land their catch. Having little money, Chandus and his brothers

Rippons Marina. *Photo by author.*

decided to deepen the channel themselves. Familiar with explosives from their service during the war, they used dynamite to blow out the channel.

"They used so much dynamite that it blew out the windows in Miss Ethel White's house," Janet laughed. "They had to replace all those windows and there were lots of them. Miss Ethel owned one of the few three-story homes on the island. Of course, they couldn't blow out a channel like that today, but back then that's the way channels were cleared. The channel for a factory on the upper island was blown out the same way. That's just the way things were done in those days. People were hard workers back then. Everything they did in those days was done by hand. It was a fascinating time."

In the 1980s, Chandus Sr. and his son, Chandus, Jr. (Channy Boy), built a 40-slip marina on the property. "Mostly watermen and transient boaters use the marina," said Janet. "We sell fuel for marine engines; both gasoline and diesel at the marina also."

Janet's mother, Charlotte Lewis Rippons, was born on the island. Her father had been a pound netter. In the early 1960s, Leon Lewis, Janet's maternal grandfather, began pound netting to supply baitfish for crabbers.

Pound nets hang from a series of poles driven into the bottom of the Bay in about fifteen feet of water. Referred to as a leader, these poles support a net that stretches from one pole to the next in a relatively straight line. The net is weighted so that it remains on the bottom of the Bay. At the end of the line of poles is a heart-shaped enclosure located in deeper water. Inside the heart is the pound, where captured fish remain. As the fish strike the net on their way up or down the Bay, their natural inclination is to retreat to deeper water. Paralleling the net, they reach the heart and pound, enter, and are trapped. The owners of the net dip the fish out of the pound with long-handled nets capable of holding three or four bushels of fish at a time.

"In the early 1970s, when I was eleven or twelve, I spent summers going with my grandfather to fish his pound nets," Janet stated. "Pop Leon had a boat named *Stewart Brothers* that he used to cross the Bay where his nets were located. The boat was sixty-five feet in length. He taught me how to steer the boat by the compass. I'd also cook for the crew of six men or so on the boat. Sometimes I'd cook up a fish that we'd caught in the net. We'd pick out the good fish like rock, bluefish, trout, spot, or flounder. The rest would be alewives (menhaden); these we'd save for bait for watermen to use in their crab pots."

Crab pots are square, box-like traps made from a type of wire that resembles chicken wire. The traps have openings on each side that allow entry for crabs. A generous supply of menhaden is stuffed into a funnel located in the bottom center of the pot. Crabs are attracted to the bait as the pot lies on the bottom of the Bay. Seeking a meal, crabs enter the pot and, after realizing they have been caught, attempt to retreat upward. The crab enters a "second story" of the pot, where there are no openings. The crabber comes along, empties the pot of crabs, rebaits it, and returns the pot, along with its line and buoy, back into the Bay, ready for another day of fishing.

Trotlining is another method that many island crabbers use to collect Maryland's most popular seafood delicacy. A lengthy line, strung between two buoys marking each end of the line, is baited every eight feet or so with chicken necks (in years gone by the bait of choice was eels). The line rests on the bottom of the river. Attracted to the bait, the crab hangs on as the line is gently lifted by the boat's momentum. As the line nears the surface, the waterman deftly separates the crab from the line with his net and it is captured.

Janet was on the *Stewart Brothers* the day the boom fell on her grandfather. "One summer day we left the dock before daybreak," Janet explained. "Pop Leon was planning to pull up the net to clean it. The boom (a 22-foot-long, heavy, pole-like appendage) was rigged so that it could assist in pulling the heavy net out of the water. In the process of pulling up the net, a block on the boom broke. I was in the galley working and everything became still and quiet. I looked up forward and saw Uncle Lem swing over onto our boat from his boat, *Sterling*, that was tied alongside us. The boom was lying on Pop's shoulder; you couldn't get a finger between his face and the boom. Capt. Joe Taylor cut the rope to the hoisting engine so it wouldn't wind Pop Leon up into it. It was an awful sight. Pop lay there unconscious; I thought he was dead.

"Men from the University of Maryland Solomons Island Biological Laboratory were aboard to tag and release fish. Pop was placed on a board full of fish scales and transferred to the Laboratory's boat. They took him to Solomons, where an ambulance was waiting to take him to the hospital in Prince Frederick. I went on the boat with Pop. He regained consciousness before we reached Solomons. I wasn't allowed to go to the hospital, so I stayed at the Lab and waited for mom and my grandmother. It was a long wait, but the hardest part was seeing the ambulance take my Pop away. He was in the hospital for a long time, but he finally got better."

Many days, after returning to shore from a day of fishing with her grandfather, she'd help her uncle, Lemuel Lewis (Pop's son), deliver menhaden to crabbers on the island. "It was a lot of fun to ride in the back of the truck," Janet said. "I'd meet people from the upper island. We had a great time."

From the time she was very young, Janet was always around the seafood plant. There was always something exciting going on there. One time she pedaled to the factory on her

Picking room. *Photo by author.*

tricycle. "I rode down the ramp in the picking room and turned the tricycle over," Janet said. "Pop took me to Mom-Mom Louise (his wife) and, after tending to my scrapes, took me home. Pop explained to me that I was too little to ride my tricycle in the factory." To Janet, the factory was, and remains, a lively and enjoyable place to be.

Like Janet, her father, Chandus, Jr., grew up in the business. One of his duties was driving a truck to Baltimore each day, delivering crabs to restaurants and retail establishments. Occasionally, trucks would make a run to Ocean City, delivering crabs to the many restaurants in the resort town. "Dad used crushed ice from the cooler to ice down the crabs," Janet explained. "He used a shovel to place the ice near the bushel baskets of live crabs in such a way that the fresh water wouldn't drip down on them and kill them. He was very particular with the way he iced down the crabs. That was before we had refrigerated trucks. Pop Chandus saw no need for refrigerated trucks. Dad had to do a lot of talking to buy the first one. After we got refrigerated trucks, delivering crabs was a whole lot easier. Daddy would leave for Baltimore at 4 or 5 in the afternoon with a load of crabs. Sometimes it'd be 4 or 5 a.m. before he finally returned home again. After I got older, I'd ride in the truck with dad on his trips to the city.

"Penny, my sister, spent more time on the truck with daddy than I did. Penny was driving the six-wheeled Ford 'pug nosed' truck and they had just crossed the Bay

Chand Sr. and Jr. *Courtesy of Janet Rippons Ruark.*

Bridge. There was a stop light at the foot of the bridge and daddy was asleep. It was in the very early morning hours and it was raining. The light turned red and Penny hit the brakes. The rear of the truck started to come around to the front. Daddy woke up and very gently told Penny, 'Give her a little gas, bare down on the air horn, and go on through the light.' He was a great teacher. He had lots of patience.

"On another trip to Baltimore in the pug nose, as Penny and dad were exiting the Harbor Tunnel, Penny looked at her father and exclaimed, 'Daddy, the tire is on fire.' Always an optimist, daddy replied, 'No, it can't be.' After coming through the tunnel, daddy got out and the tire was, indeed, on fire. He reached for a fire extinguisher and aimed it at the tire. A car had also stopped and a man jumped out with a six-pack of beer. He shook the beer and the cans sprayed beer all over the tire. That beer put out the fire faster than the fire extinguisher."

Penny, who is three years younger than Janet, their mother, and great-grandmother, Lessie, all worked in the factory picking crabs. "I never picked crabs, but I did pull off the shells after they were steamed in order for the pickers to get out the meat," she said.

Janet's brother, C. T., also worked in the seafood business, delivering product. Currently making his home in Colorado, he still manages to help his mother with the book work. "He challenges mom's computer skills," Janet stated. "Mom says he keeps her brain active."

Janet attended elementary school on the upper island. Three teachers were assigned to the school. Each teacher taught two grade levels. First and second grades were grouped together, as were third and fourth and fifth and sixth. For grades seven through ten, she attended South Dorchester High School in Golden Hill, about ten miles from the island. Her final two years of school were spent at the new Cambridge South Dorchester High School, which opened in 1976.

Following graduation from high school in 1978, Janet commuted daily to Cambridge for a job in an automotive parts business. "I just loved my boss," she said. "He was just like my grandfather Chand. He had a great sense of humor and he was always kidding around.

"My grandfather's sense of humor was legendary. In 1980, when a new $3.5 million bridge was built that joined upper and middle island, County Commissioner Thomas

A. Flowers (a Hoopers Island native) offered a prayer during the dedication ceremony. During his prayer, he called the bridge 'a monument to man's stupidity.' The next evening, Walter Cronkite reported the incident and referred to the bridge as 'a bridge to nowhere.' Someone asked my grandfather what he thought of Cronkite's comments. After thinking for a moment, my grandfather said, 'Bridge to nowhere — that depends on which way you're headed.'

"Pop Chand always said that a crab was the most patriotic animal there is. The underside of the male crab has the shape of the Washington Monument and the underside of the female, the shape of the U. S. Capitol Building.

"He always said that he'd never met a stranger. He was well regarded by everybody and he returned that affection to all."

In 1979, after she and Clarence Ruark were married, her father asked her to join him in helping run the business. "My grandfather was getting older and daddy wanted him to take it easy," she said. "I came that year and I've been here ever since."

Since her father's death in 2006, Janet has been in charge of the business. "Daddy was at the factory with us just a couple of hours before he died," she explained. "He had gone home for lunch and to take a nap. He never awakened from his nap. The next morning, I picked up the employees and we all hugged and comforted each other. At 3:30 a.m., I opened the office door. His favorite pen was where he had left it and his chair was empty. I opened my Bible in search of strength. In the stillness of the morning, I read Psalm 32-8. 'The Lord said…I will instruct you and teach you in the way you should go. I will counsel you and watch over you.' I knew, after reading these words, everything would be all right."

With the exception of book work, which her mother does, Janet does a little bit of everything around the factory. "Whatever needs to be done, I do it," she said. "Clarence does all the mechanical work that is needed. He's a big help.

Bridge to nowhere. *Photo by author*.

"We have about twenty-five crab pickers working here now. In the old days, pickers were all from the island. Many have gotten too old to do the work or have died off. The ones that are of working age have found jobs in town (Cambridge). There are also a lot of people who have moved here from away. If they need work, they usually want full-time rather than seasonal work like we do here.

"In 1996, we were able to bring up some pickers from Mexico. They come here for the crabbing season that begins April 1 and runs until November 15. Last season we had twenty-five of them working here. They are hard workers — they work just like my mom and my grandmother worked. It's hard to judge how many pickers you'll need because the catch fluctuates so much. No two years are alike. One year might be very good and the next could be terrible. It is cyclical. It's always been that way. We've been blessed, though, to stay in business as long as we have."

Janet's work day begins at 4 a.m. "There's nothing like getting up in the still of the morning," she said. "It seems like you're closer to God at that time of day. I love getting up early. We pick crabs until noon time. All the employees work very hard."

A few years ago, seafood packers were in jeopardy of losing their Mexican employees. The government places a quota on the number of foreign workers who come into the country and, because seafood is a seasonal business, by the time pickers are needed in the spring, the quota has usually been filled and processors were threatened with losing their workers. U. S. Senator Barbara Mikulski (D-Md.) fought to save the industry and, through her efforts, packers retained their workers. "Senator Mikulski really saved the crabbing industry in Maryland," said Janet. "She has been a valuable friend."

Rippons Brothers Seafood processes about seventy-five bushels of crabs each day during the crabbing season. Crabs are bought from local watermen who land their catch on the Rippons docks. After landing the crabs, they are taken to a steamer that has the capability of cooking twenty-five to thirty bushels at a time. After steaming, the crabs are taken to the picking room, where the meat is separated from the outer shell and packed in containers for shipment.

In addition to the local watermen who supply the plant with crabs, a boat owned by the business makes a daily trip to Smith Island. About fifteen to twenty Smith Island crabbers sell their catch to the Rippons facility daily during crabbing season.

The *Rippons Lady* is forty feet long and powered by a large diesel engine. Janet's husband, Clarence, captains the boat for its hour-plus run to and from the island. The *Rippons Lady* has transported as many as three hundred bushels of crabs on one run from Smith back to Hoopers Island. Two other boats were used before the *Rippons Lady*; the *Lessie I* and *Lessie II* made the daily trips to the island for many years prior to the *Rippons Lady's* acquisition and were named for Chandus, Sr.'s mother.

"Sometimes I worry about Clarence out there on the Bay," Janet said. "He goes out in just about any type of weather and it is often very rough and stormy. Eddie Evans has been like a father to Clarence ever since his dad died when he was young. Eddie told me one time that Clarence takes some awful chances coming up that Bay. Sometimes I'll tell him that it's too rough and he should stay home. Dad told him the same thing one time. Clarence told daddy that he was the captain of the boat and it was his decision whether to go or not. 'If I'm going to be scared out there,' he told daddy, 'it's time to get off the water.' Pop Leon told me that Clarence has been on the Bay since he was in diapers. 'Clarence knows what he's doing,' he said. 'Don't worry about him; he knows the Bay and what the boat will stand.'"

Clarence Ruark comes from a large Hoopers Island family and is well aware of the dangers of his profession. "Pop Leon often told me he would tell his oldest son, Leon, Jr., 'Now son, if it's too rough for Cosh Ruark (Clarence's father) to go out on the Bay, then

Janet beside the crab steamer. *Photo by author*.

you can stay ashore," Janet said. "Pop Leon said Clarence's father was a fine waterman. He knew how to handle a boat. He passed on this knowledge to Clarence."

Despite the precautions that watermen take, accidents happen. In 1962, Leon Lewis, Jr. (age 20), his brother Lemuel (age 12), and Arvie Ruark (age 17, Clarence's older brother) left the dock for a day of crabbing. Near the Hoopers Island Lighthouse, the engine exploded. "My mother and grandmother saw the smoke and my grandmother said, 'Some mother's heart will be breaking tonight,'" Janet said. "Little did she know! Uncle Lem was the only survivor. He said they huddled together and said The Lord's Prayer after the explosion."

Watermen who venture out on the Bay must constantly be aware of the weather. Storms are frequent on the Chesapeake during the height of the summer. From late summer into fall, the threat of hurricanes is very much a reality. Some of these storms have decimated the island. In 1933, a tremendous storm came through the area. Known as the August Storm of 1933, it has, more recently, believed to have been a hurricane. "The storm had a lot of water in it and the island was flooded," said Janet. "It washed the bridge away between the middle and lower island. That's when damage occurs, when there is a lot of water in a storm. My grandfather, Leon, was part of a dredge boat crew back then and, like lots of men, he rode out the storm aboard the boat. He was able to keep the boat safe from harm.

"In 1954, a hurricane named Hazel hit the area. The winds were great, but there wasn't as much water in it as the 1933 storm. There were a lot of boats that washed out of their slips and moorings; some ended up miles away from here. Hurricane Isabel, in 2003, had both

The *Lessie II. Courtesy of Janet Rippons Ruark.*

water and a lot of wind in it. We had a pavilion next to the factory back then where people could sit and eat crabs. Isabel took that away. She did a lot of damage further north in the Bay. Hurricane Agnes, in 1972, did a lot of damage to the island. Agnes brought a lot of pollution down the Bay with her. The storm killed lots of things in the Bay. All the grasses (submerged aquatic vegetation) were gone and lots of oysters were smothered by the debris and silt the storm brought. Before Agnes, there was lots of grass out in the Honga.

"Grasses have started to make a comeback since Agnes. Just since dad died, it seems like the Bay has gotten healthier. The state used to allow dredging for oysters only by skipjacks; now dredging with power boats is allowed. This method is much more efficient. It seems like power dredging removes the silt from the oysters. It also turns them over like cultivating crops on land. All this cleans up oysters and allows them to breathe. Before dredging, many oysters died because they were smothered by the silt. Oysters have made a comeback in the Honga River and in other rivers of the Bay. That's a good sign!"

Rippons Bros., at one time, bought oysters directly from watermen as they were taken from the Bay. Oysters were not shucked or processed at the plant. Instead, they were resold after being purchased. "We haven't been involved with oysters for years because they have been so scarce," said Janet. "Who knows, if they get plentiful again we may get back into them."

Janet feels that Mother Nature is wonderfully mysterious. "It seems like if there are a lot of crabs, there won't be great numbers of fish," she said. "If there are lots of fish, there won't be many crabs. If female crabs sponge (are pregnant) in the spring, there won't be any marketable crabs until later in the summer. That's the way it is. We are totally dependent on Mother Nature for our livelihood."

Rippons Brothers Seafood remains a family business. "My daughter, Colleen, is the fifth generation of our family to work in the business," Janet said. "Like every generation of Rippons, Colleen does whatever needs to be done. She's a big help."

Janet Rippons has a strong commitment to the community in which she lives. "I come from a community that has a great big heart," she stated. "I have been truly blessed to be part of the Hoopers Island community. A community where if you're hurt or in need, there's always somebody to pick you up. This is a community where you'd never go hungry. Somebody always has something to eat and to share. This is a great place, I wouldn't trade living on this island for anything. I am very thankful for the opportunity to have lived my life as I have."

Chapter Nine

Kelley Phillips Cox

Kelley Phillips Cox traces the maternal side of her family back to the very first English settlement in the state of Maryland. Located on Kent Island, the community was the third oldest permanent settlement in the United States. Only Jamestown and Plymouth were founded earlier.

In 1631, English immigrant William Claiborne traveled north in the Chesapeake from his base in Jamestown and established a trading post on the island for the purpose of trading with Native Americans. Named for his birthplace in England, he called the settlement, and the island on which it was located, Fort Kent Manor. Eventually, a small community of approximately one hundred populated Claiborne's trading post.

Having laid claim to his settlement and the island on which it was located, Claiborne's actions soon came to the attention of Cecil Calvert, the second Lord Baltimore, who had been given a charter establishing the colony of Maryland. Since he purchased the island from Native Americans, Claiborne felt the island to be rightfully his. Thereafter, a ten-year conflict between Claiborne and Calvert ensued. In the end, Calvert was victorious and Claiborne was forced to relinquish any claims he had for the island.

Many of the settlers at Claiborne's Trading Post had immigrated to Jamestown as indentured servants. Among them were Kelley's ancestors. "After Calvert recalled Tilghman, he returned to England," said Kelley. "While Tilghman was back in England, the indentured servants scampered away. Among them were my ancestors."

Kelley's ancestors eventually made their way to an island further south, later to be known as Tilghman, and settled there. "My ancestors' names were Cummins," Kelley continued. "One of the first land owners on Tilghman Island was a family named Phillips. In 1829, one of the Phillips's descendants married a descendant from my maternal side. Seven generations ago my ancestors settled on Tilghman and we've been part of this community ever since."

The younger of two daughters, Kelley has lived on Tilghman Island for the majority of her fifty-two years. "My dad was a waterman named Garland Phillips," Kelley explained. "He was a Tilghman Island native. My mom, Adrienne, was originally from Easton." When she was born, Kelley was premature; June was the month she was expected to arrive, however, she was born in April. "Perhaps that's why I'm impatient," she laughed. "I'm always early for appointments and meetings."

In addition to working the waters of the Chesapeake Bay, Garland owned waterfront property on a slender stretch of water that separates Tilghman from the mainland. Known as Knapps Narrows, it is an area where a sizable fleet of workboats are moored. A couple of marinas also line the waterway. On his property, Garland operated a crab business, locally known as Phillips Wharf. The family lived nearby. "From the time I was very young, I was involved in the seafood business," said Kelley. "We shedded and sold soft crabs and spent lots of time working on crab pots. I knew, from a very early age, that I didn't want to be involved with harvesting seafood. From the age of eight or nine, all I wanted to be was a marine biologist."

In February 1979, when Kelley was sixteen years old, her father drowned. "Dad was fishing out in the Bay and it was very, very cold," she said. "We don't really know exactly what happened, but it is believed that as dad was backing the boat down to pick up the fishing net it got wound around the propellers. The net was so frozen and heavy with ice that it dragged the stern of the boat underwater and it sank immediately. There were five family members on the boat that day and all were lost. In addition to my father, two cousins were later found tangled in the net. Dad's uncle and his son were also aboard. All the bodies were recovered fairly quickly, except my father's. Months after the accident, his body was found in Maryland's southern portion of the Bay. Dad's boat was named *Hey Russ IV*. She was a brand new, fifty-foot, fiberglass boat with scuppers to let out any water that washed up on deck. Presumably, the scuppers iced over and didn't allow the water to escape as it should." Garland Phillips was forty-seven years old when he died.

During her elementary and secondary school years, Kelley took every opportunity to involve herself in activities that related to marine biology. Following graduation from St. Michaels High School in 1980, she matriculated at the University of North Carolina in Wilmington, North Carolina. "That was just too much ocean for me," she said. "I was interested in the Chesapeake." Returning closer to home, she enrolled at Salisbury State University, where, in 1984, she earned a degree in biology with a minor in chemistry. While a Salisbury student, she did field work at the University of Maryland Research facility at Horn Point, just outside of Cambridge. "I worked in the oyster hatchery there as well as on a research vessel," she said.

After graduation, Kelley's first job was mate on a research vessel based at the Chesapeake Bay Biological Laboratory in Solomon's. Shortly after that, she worked at a laboratory in Benedict, Maryland, that was owned by the Philadelphia Academy of Sciences. She was involved with fish propagation at the lab. Studying rockfish, she and other scientists examined their feeding habits and how sedimentation in the Bay affected the ability of the young fish to see the food supply. "Although I enjoyed my job, the lab was operated on soft money (grant money)," she said. "Because of this, my future there was uncertain. My feeling was that when the money ran out, my job would no longer be available."

An opportunity came along for Kelley to be a park ranger. Desiring the security of a state position, she was stationed at the state park at Point Lookout in the southern portion of the state. She was employed there for a year.

"In the mid-1980s, a lot of funding came along for Chesapeake Bay clean up," Kelley stated. "I worked out of Annapolis in a state field office, which, at the time, was run by the State of Maryland Department of Health. I spent ten years there collecting data for the Chesapeake Bay Program. We went all over the state conducting water quality studies. We'd test water quality near sewage treatment plants before and again after the plants were upgraded as a result of the Governor's Initiative. In this way, we could ascertain if the plant was in better condition than it was before the upgrades."

Kelley also collected samples from the Bay aboard a research vessel. "We collected specimens from Smith Point in the southern Bay to Havre de Grace in the north," she said. "We were on the vessel three days every other week collecting samples."

Married since 1987 to Jerry Cox, a Calvert County native and captain of a research vessel, Kelley, in 1994, underwent major heart surgery. The surgery was very serious and involved rerouting her blood. The operation left her unable to perform her job duties.

Leaving state employment, Kelley and Jerry returned to Tilghman in 1992 and operated a water taxi business. People who were anchored in nearby creeks aboard their boats would call and request a ride to one of the many restaurants or other attractions in Tilghman. "We'd go and pick them up. Later we'd return them to their anchored boats," Kelley said. "Business grew and we added a second boat to serve the town of Oxford. We also bought a passenger van with which we served patrons from area hotels as far away as St. Michaels. We even had the pleasure of transporting Margaret Thatcher. We were really afraid of the liability of what we were doing. We worked long hours and, many times, we transported inebriated people. We were burned out."

While vacationing on Hilton Head Island, Kelley and Jerry noticed a 33-foot boat that was being used for dolphin tours. It was a former U. S. Navy utility boat that held around twenty-nine passengers. The couple later learned the boat was for sale. Returning to Hilton Head, they bought the boat and renamed it the *Express Princess*. Docking the boat in St. Michaels, they utilized it for ecology and sunset cruises. A few years later, they purchased a larger boat, a fifty-footer, that they named the *Express Royale*. It had also been a former Navy boat. Jerry redid the entire boat and, ultimately, it was certified by the U. S. Coast Guard to carry forty-nine passengers. This boat enabled the couple to take larger groups on cruises.

In 2003, Hurricane Isabel whirled through the area, creating havoc and leaving destruction in her wake. The extremely high water that accompanied the hurricane did major damage to low lying areas like Tilghman Island. The entire wharf where the family business had operated was wiped out. By 2005, Kelley and Jerry had built back the wharf and also added a building that housed an environmental center. The following year, the center was granted non-profit status.

At the Phillips Wharf Environmental Center, Kelley began conducting environmental education programs for children and adults. In 2009, a fishmobile was added. A converted bus, the fishmobile contains a variety of live specimens from the Chesapeake. Turtles, horseshoe crabs, sea horses, and fish, among others, are displayed in aquariums. Kelley allows many of the animals to be touched if the visitor desires. The fishmobile enables Kelley and staff to travel to schools and other locations, displaying some of the animals that reside in the Chesapeake. It is her hope that, through these activities, children and adults will have a greater appreciation for the Chesapeake Bay. "Approximately 8,000 to 10,000 people go through the fishmobile each year," Kelley explained.

Phillips Wharf Building. *Photo by author.*

The *EXPRESS ROYALE*. *Photo by author.*

Fishmobile. *Photo by author.*

In addition to the fishmobile, the Center offers a variety of programs for children and adults. "Ninth graders in Talbot County are involved in a fisheries management unit," said Kelley. "We focus on menhaden. We take them out in the boat and they observe watermen retrieving fish from pound nets and, later, we'll have classroom exercises based on that experience. We discuss the declining fishery and what that means to the Bay and to the watermen. Menhaden, like oysters, are filter feeders. If their numbers were increased, this would help clean the Bay's waters."

Fourth graders are exposed to an oyster module. For that experience, students are taken out on a skipjack and witness the oyster dredging process. "They even get to dissect an oyster," said Kelley.

A summer program is offered that involves studying the life of the crab. "The kids go out trotlining with a professional crabber," said Kelley. "We discuss the crabbing industry and the life cycle of the crab. Between five hundred and six hundred kids are involved in this program during a summer."

Another program offered at Phillips Wharf is Marylanders Grow Oysters. Citizens who live on waterfront properties are issued cages in which spat (young oysters) are placed. The spat that is used comes from the laboratory at Horn Point. Cages are suspended from the docks of participants, who maintain the cages. In about a year, the cages are collected and the oysters are removed and taken to an oyster sanctuary in a nearby creek for further growth.

"There are ninety growers in our program," Kelley explained. "We do diagnostics and mortality studies on our oysters to determine if diseases are present. We found that our oysters are relatively healthy. Years ago a disease called dermo infiltrated oyster beds in the Chesapeake. The waters around Tilghman were a hot bed for dermo. Last year there was very

Kelley holding oysters. *Photo by author.*

little dermo in our oysters. We are thinking that oysters are beginning to develop some resistance to the condition. If true, this is really a good discovery. This project is a really good citizen science program. We had some really good oysters at the end of the season last year."

On the grounds of the Environmental Center is a project involving conservation landscaping. "We put in a buffer area near our parking lot," Kelley stated. "The idea is that our parking lot will drain into the buffer garden we have installed and the plants will take off the toxins from the runoff and only clean water will enter the Narrows."

Another project of Phillips Wharf is the oyster house project. There is an oyster-processing facility sitting next to the Narrows, not far from Phillips Wharf. There has been some sort of seafood processing house in that location since the early 1900s. The property is for sale and Kelley would very much like to acquire it. "We'd move our operation down there," she said. "There is a large metal building on the grounds that we could convert into classroom and office space. It is also large enough to house the exhibit area for our animals. The processing house that is on the water we would use as a shucking facility. We anticipate contracting that part of the project out to a professional seafood packer. Fresh seafood would be sold from there and oysters and crabs would be processed there. We hope to have a wall of glass through which visitors could view the seafood as it is being processed. We are hopeful that it will happen. We'd like to keep Tilghman as a legacy destination. We feel that it would be an attraction for tourists."

Estimating that it will take a million and a half dollars to complete the facility, Kelley and her Board have already raised half of the asking price of $500,000. "We hope to have the funding to close on the property by next October," she stated. "We are confident that we'll find the remaining funds to buy the facility by that time."

Kelley is very interested in aquaculture and sees that as the answer for Chesapeake watermen. "There just is not enough wild harvest out there to support the industry," she said. "Aquaculture (the process of growing seafood in other than a natural state) would augment the wild harvest. There are a couple of businesses nearby that are using aquaculture to grow oysters and the resultant product looks promising. In fact, the oysters grown by one company were voted the top oyster at a trade show in Boston recently. Our watermen haven't bought into the concept yet though. As soon as someone makes a profit from aquaculture, I'm hopeful they'll buy into the concept."

Kelley feels that some state initiatives have been successful. "Over the years, some efforts at Bay clean-up have been positive," she said. "When I worked with the state, phosphate reduction was a big effort. Phosphate was banned from detergents and it made a big difference in water quality. The moratorium on catching female crabs has had good results. The blue crab industry is the only thing that is keeping our watermen afloat, economically, right now. That was an experiment that made a positive impact. Menhaden and oysters

Proposed new location of Phillips Wharf.
Photo by author.

are the keys to a healthier, cleaner Bay. They both filter the water. Anything we can do to enhance their numbers is a good thing."

There are programs that must be initiated if the Bay is, once again, ever to reach a healthier state. "The Bay has a long way to go, however," Kelley said. "In many localities, storm water runs off into the Bay untreated. This water is full of toxins that are harmful to the Bay. Storm water should be collected and siphoned off. If allowed to collect in sewage treatment plants, it'll overwhelm the system and cause overflows. Of course, overflows end up directly in the tributaries. More needs to be done in this regard."

Kelley feels that there may be some questionable budgetary practices in Annapolis. "The last Governor imposed a flush tax on landowners," she stated. "Funds that resulted from this were to be used to upgrade sewage treatment plants. With the exception of a few upgrades early on, we don't really know where those funds have since been spent. Politicians don't talk about it because those dollars are probably being spent for things other than sewage treatment upgrades.

"Sewage treatment plants are, in actuality, only a drop in the bucket compared to the nitrogen that is emitted by vehicle exhaust and other sources. Nitrogen filters back down from the atmosphere and much of it collects in the Chesapeake Bay. Nitrogen is also a factor in sewage treatment. Any new septic installation is required to include denitrofication as a part of the system. This is a good thing, but it adds roughly twice the cost to the installation."

Farmers currently receive a lot of the blame for the Chesapeake's imbalance, according to Kelley. "Farming today is very high tech," she said. "Farmers use GPS and computers to research the amount of nutrients that their fields require to be productive. They don't over-fertilize like in the old days. Private landowners, on the other hand, have really become a problem. Homeowners who live near the watershed are free to apply as much fertilizer as they want in order to get a greener lawn. Experts tell us that private landowners apply five times more fertilizer than needed to their lawns. Yards only should be fertilized once a year, in the fall. Application at other times is a waste. Fertilizer just runs off into the watershed. Landscapers enhance the problem. They, of course, advocate fertilizing several times a year. They don't agree that the practices they condone contribute to the Chesapeake's problems. There is a fanaticism among homeowners to have the greenest lawn in the neighborhood. We haven't been able to convince them of their harmful practices. This is a problem we don't have a handle on."

Pet waste is another problem area that goes unchecked, according to Kelley. "People who live near the water have a tendency to throw pet waste overboard," she said. "In the upper Bay, most of the beach closures in recent years have resulted from inappropriate discarding of pet waste."

The introduction of non-native plants is another difficulty. "Imported plants tend to grow more quickly than native species," said Kelley. "We've recently introduced non-native plants from Asia. Our native insects, butterflies, etc. aren't attracted to them. There is a good chance that imported plants bring with them parasites and other insects about which we have little knowledge."

Kelley feels the Conowingo Dam on the Susquehanna River may be today's biggest threat to the health of the Bay. "I fear the day when all that sediment that is piled up behind the dam overflows into the main stem of the Bay," she said. "We must have a containment project upstream of the dam to collect it before it comes downstream. When it does come down, there will be no living things left in the wake of all that sediment."

Some recent political mandates baffle Kelley. "Maryland has recently declared to reduce the catch limits for menhaden in the Bay," she said. "The catch is to be reduced by 20% beginning this summer. This is not a good thing. Maryland only harvests 1 to 1-1/2% of the total East Coast menhaden catch. We catch so few menhaden in Maryland that we shouldn't have catch limits imposed. Catch limits could easily ruin our crabbing industry. Crab Potters use menhaden for bait. The supply may be seriously reduced. At best, the cost of menhaden will be prohibitive, but crabbers will probably continue to be paid only as much as they traditionally received for their product from processors. My fear is that many of them will be unable to make a living from crabbing as a result."

Kelley is very concerned about the future of the watermen of the Chesapeake Bay. Only a few Chesapeake watermen make a decent living by today's standards, Kelley feels. "The watermen that do well must be willing to work 24/7 today," she said. "Watermen feel the state has no regard for the manner by which they earn a living. They feel the state is running them out of business. They resent the mandates that are forced upon them and feel they have no voice or recourse in Annapolis. As a result, their numbers are dwindling. In 2000, there were 6,000 to 8,000 licensed watermen in the state. Now only half that number work Maryland's waters. Tilghman Island currently only has thirty or forty full-time licensed watermen. At one time, everyone on the island was either a waterman or a farmer. Most of them are getting along in years. There are very few youngsters coming along. With regulations being imposed by the state, the waterman's life is not getting any easier. It is a difficult way to make a living. For them to earn a decent living today, they must have a terrific work ethic. The watermen want the same things as the environmentalists — a clean Chesapeake Bay.

"I come from generations of watermen and I am fearful for the life of the watermen. When they die off, a whole heritage and culture that is unique to the Chesapeake will die with them. It will be a shame to lose that beautiful part of our history."

CHAPTER TEN

Margaret Sherman Bryan

"The doctor that brought me into this world had an interesting name," Margaret Sherman Bryan laughed. "His name was Dr. Hope. Very few people had a car in those days, but Dr. Hope owned one and he made house calls. He also delivered babies. He delivered babies right in the home. We lived in a village named Claiborne and I guess Dr. Hope delivered most of the babies there in the same manner. I was delivered ninety years ago."

Located five miles west of St. Michaels, Claiborne was a very active community when Margaret was growing up. "There were no more than a hundred or so people living in Claiborne in those days," she explained. "There were two general stores, a post office, a church, and a one-room school that had grades 1 through 4. The school was staffed by one teacher. Just about everybody who lived in town was associated with the Claiborne-Annapolis Ferry. We had deck hands, cooks, captains, mechanics, and other folks who worked on the ferry living in town then."

Claiborne was the southern terminus for the ferry that ran from the village to the state capital, Annapolis, on the opposite shores of the Chesapeake Bay. Subsidized by state funds, the Claiborne-Annapolis Ferry began service in 1919. Each trip was an hour and twenty minutes in duration.

Prior to being served by the ferry, Claiborne had been a landing for steamboats since the 1890s. Steamboats traveled to Chesapeake tributaries from Baltimore and supplied an abundance of goods required by citizens in rural areas. The ships also served as a major transportation mode for passengers as they traveled from one town to another. "The Chesapeake Bay separated the western and eastern sides of the state and the Bay was the highway people used as a means to get from place to place," said Margaret. "Steamboats were the primary vehicles that traveled that highway system."

In Claiborne, steamers connected with a railroad that took passengers as far south as Ocean City, the sole ocean resort in the state. The Pennsylvania Railroad Company

Claiborne Ferry dock. *Courtesy of Margaret Sherman Bryan.*

owned the railroad and it operated under the name Baltimore, Claiborne and Atlantic Railway. "Those familiar with the railroad called it the B. C. and A. and nicknamed it Black Cinders and Ashes," Margaret smiled.

Railroad stations were all over the Eastern Shore in those days. Every small town had a station. There were not many cars and the few roads available were in deplorable condition. Many times the roads were impassable. Railroads, steamboats, and, later, ferries provided the major connections to the outside world.

Margaret's father was B. Frank Sherman. In 1919, Sherman began his tenure with the ferry service as a ticket agent. Decorated for bravery while fighting in France during World War I, he was good friends with the son of the 48th Governor of Maryland, Emerson C. Harrington. Formerly of Cambridge, Harrington was instrumental in Sherman's appointment. Frank, the son of the widowed Dorchester County Sheriff, had lived in Cambridge during his youth. During the twelve years his dad was sheriff, he and his father lived in private living quarters at the county jail.

"Only one ferry served the Claiborne-Annapolis line when daddy began his employment," Margaret said. "The ferry was a steam-powered, walking beam, side-wheeler named the *Governor Emerson C. Harrington*. Governor Harrington's wife christened the newly-rebuilt ferry during the dedication ceremonies and the Governor made appropriate remarks. Following that, the *Governor Emerson C. Harrington's* lines were cast off for its initial trip to Claiborne. Waiting on the dock in Claiborne was my dad."

The *Harrington* was not a double-ender like most of today's ferries. Cars were loaded from the side of the vessel; once inside, they were positioned appropriately for the trip across the Bay. About 10,000 vehicles a year used the ferry system, each car paying a $2 fee.

Despite this apparent success, by 1921, the Claiborne-Annapolis Ferry was experiencing financial difficulties and bankruptcy resulted. By then, Governor Harrington's term was over and he turned his attention to reorganizing the ferry line. John M. Dennis, President of the Union Trust Bank, was a major financial backer and supporter. Former Governor Harrington was eventually named President of the newly formed Claiborne-Annapolis Ferry, Inc.

"The reorganized system proved successful and business increased," Margaret stated. "In 1924, my father was named the General Manager of the company and, in 1926, a second ferry, the *Albert C. Ritchie*, was added. The *Ritchie* was nearly two hundred feet long and could carry seventy-five cars. She was made of wood and was the first double-ended ferry to travel the Chesapeake. In 1929, a third ferry was added, the *John M. Dennis*. The *Dennis* was over two hundred feet in length and had a capacity of sixty-five cars and nearly nine hundred passengers.

"After daddy was named General Manager, his office was in Annapolis. He'd ride the morning ferry to his office each day and return home on the 6 p.m. run. There were hardships and ferries made dangerous crossings from time to time.

"As the ferry neared the landing in Claiborne one day, the captain yelled down to my dad, who was standing on the dock, and asked, 'What side of the dock do you want this ferry to sink on?' There was a hole in the side of the ferry and water was pouring in. Daddy told one of the ferry employees that he would buy him a new uniform if he would jump in and stuff blankets in the hole. The employee did as asked and the ferry survived. My dad later bought him a new uniform.

"One night, in 1925, a woman passenger who was holding a baby fell into the water as she was leaving the ferry. The woman was quickly rescued, but the baby was not seen. A short time later, someone noticed the baby floating, peacefully, face up and unharmed. They reached down, picked up the bundle, and the baby was fine.

"In 1933, a horrific storm hit the Eastern Shore. If a storm like that hit today, it would be called a hurricane. Our family was all safely gathered at home as the storm whirled through the area. The phone rang and someone told daddy that the *Gov. Albert C. Ritchie* was in trouble as she laid in her slip at the ferry dock at Matapeake. Daddy was told that the storm had driven her on top of a piling and she was listing badly. It was feared that, with a lowering of the tide, the ferry might overturn. Daddy got into his car, made the trip to Matapeake, and surveyed the situation. He instructed workers to cut a hole in the ferry's deck so she could fall with the tide. The crew did as he asked and the ferry survived the storm with no other damage. Later, representatives from the insurance firm refused to reimburse the state for repairs to the vessel. Daddy told them that if the hole hadn't been made in the decking, the whole ferry would have been lost and the company would've had to pay a whole lot more. With that, the insurance company settled."

The Claiborne-Annapolis Ferry was extremely important and, because of its role as the eastern terminus for the ferry, the town of Claiborne prospered. The ferry's influence spread to the surrounding area as well. Small boarding houses sprang up that catered to city dwellers wishing to get away. Near Claiborne was Wade's Point and Safety Beach. Maple Hall was located in Claiborne.

"When the ferry arrived, Claiborne became a very busy town," Margaret said. "Our house was situated on a bend and offered a good view of the ferries when they came in

108

to the dock. After the ferry was secured, we could clearly see the cars as they came off the ferry and proceeded through the town. One of our favorite pastimes was to sit on our big, screened porch and identify the make of cars as they left the ferry. Often there would be lines of traffic going through our little town. After unloading, we'd watch the ferry as it made its way back out into the Bay for the return trip to Annapolis. It was exciting!

"Living in Claiborne was a good life. Growing up, we roller-skated, swam, ice-skated on the ponds in winter, and rode our bikes. There was no booze or drugs and we had no car. Mine was a great childhood. Our house was very busy. In addition to my dad and mother, Ethel, Daddy's father, George Sherman, lived with us and also my maternal grandmother, Anna Harrison. Our house was not large; lots of people today wouldn't understand how three different families could survive under one roof like we did. In those days, families took in older relatives. There were no nursing homes and retirement places like there are now. That's just the way things were back then. We all got along and were happy.

"For the first four years of schooling, I attended the one-room school in town. Each student was assigned a wooden desk with a chair attached. The desks ranged in size from very small for the youngest students to large ones on the opposite side of the room. Large desks were used by fourth graders. The teacher's desk was in the front of the room and the blackboards were behind her. There was a coal stove in the room to keep us warm in winter and a line of windows were on one wall, which were opened in warmer months. There was an outhouse behind the school building with separate accommodations for boys and girls. A belfry was attached to the roof and the bell would ring when recess was over. I enjoyed school very much.

"In fifth grade, we transferred to St. Michaels High School. There were only eleven grades back then and we were transported to school by bus. Our bus had a wooden body and there were benches along both sides. Our driver would ask us to move to one side, on occasion, when the gas tank was running low. I really enjoyed high school. I was active in drama and was the newspaper editor in high school. There were many more students there and they came from different parts of the county. The boy who would eventually become my husband was a classmate. His name was Philip Beverly Bryan; he went by his middle name. Reminiscent of the song, 'A Boy Named Sue,' Bev's name would cause him a good deal of aggravation as he went through life."

The Claiborne-Annapolis route was altered in 1938. No longer did ferries travel from Claiborne to Annapolis. Instead, they traveled from Claiborne to a new terminal at Romancoke, on the southern tip of Kent Island, further north on the Eastern Shore. During the dedication of the new terminal, fifteen-year-old Margaret not only cut the ribbon, but also officiated at the ceremony. From Romancoke, cars drove five miles to another new terminal at Matapeake, where they boarded another ferry for the trip across the Bay.

In 1941, the state purchased the ferry company and renamed it the Chesapeake Bay Ferry System. Plans were underway to replace the ferry with a bridge. By then, additional ferries had been added to the fleet. A large ferry, the *Governor Herbert R. O'Connor* had a capacity of seventy-five vehicles and over eight hundred passengers. Also added was the *Gov. Harry Nice*; at two hundred feet, she could carry sixty-eight cars and nearly eight hundred passengers. At 146 feet, the *Eastern Bay* was the smallest vessel in the fleet. These vessels joined the *Governor Emerson Harrington II* (a replacement for the original *Harrington*), *John M. Dennis*, and *Albert C. Ritchie*.

A new terminal was opened on the western side of the Bay at Sandy Point. Thereafter, the Annapolis terminal, which had been located in the downtown area, adjacent to the Naval Academy wall, was closed.

Dedication announcements. *Courtesy of Margaret Sherman Bryan.*

In 1948, the Maryland Senate passed a resolution allowing the ferry *Eastern Bay* to be renamed the *B. Frank Sherman.* "Daddy was quite proud and honored when this happened," Margaret said. "The *B. Frank Sherman* was built in 1926. The diesel powered vessel had a capacity of thirty-three cars and five hundred passengers."

Following graduation from high school in 1940, Margaret matriculated at the University of Maryland, College Park. "It was a lot different than anything I was used to," Margaret said. "I was just a country girl. The women's dorm seemed enormous, but I enjoyed the college experience. I majored in history and languages. I was thinking about going into the Foreign Service, but the war broke out and changed everything. I remember vividly where I was when I heard the news that we were at war. I was in my second year at the University. I had moved from the dorm to the Gamma Phi Beta sorority house on campus, where I would live for the next two years. We were having dinner and one of the girls announced that we were at war with Japan. I was eighteen years old and, until then, had lived a sheltered life, insulated from many of society's problems. The war hastened my maturity. Patriotism was pervasive. We all wanted to contribute to the war effort.

"Many young men immediately volunteered to join the military. By 1942, women were permitted to join the military. They weren't allowed in combat, but one of my sorority sisters left college to fly airplanes from Canada to Greenland, where they were then flown to England for use in Europe. My parents encouraged me to remain at the University and finish my studies.

"We had classes year-round after 1941; there were no more summer breaks. Everything was chaotic in those days. All the students had to take courses related to the war. Some took first aid, some enrolled in sewing classes. Some of the girls I knew became

The B. FRANK SHERMAN. *Courtesy of Margaret Sherman Bryan.*

'Rosie the Riveter' in war manufacturing plants. I took a course in diffusing incendiary bombs. We were sure Washington, D.C. was going to be bombed and our campus was just a few miles away. We took turns being Wardens during blackouts and walked around campus, making sure blinds were drawn and no lights were on. On weekends, we'd go to Washington and visit the U.S.O., dance, and socialize with the troops.

"Our lifestyle was drastically changed due to the war. Ration stamps were issued for meat, sugar, clothing, and a host of other things. Gasoline was also rationed, as were tires. Factories were transformed for the war effort and manufactured tanks, airplanes, and other military equipment.

"Our junior prom, in 1942, was held in Washington at the Wardman Park Hotel. The University arranged for several streetcars to come to the campus and transport us to the prom. It was amusing to watch all the students get on and off the streetcars in their formal attire. We had to adjust, it was wartime."

Following graduation in December 1943, Margaret lived in Silver Spring, Maryland, and worked at a variety of temporary jobs. Bev Bryan and Margaret had stayed in touch through the years by letters and infrequent visits. In 1942, Bev joined the Coast Guard and was sent to Florida. "Bev joined the Coast Guard because he enjoyed small boats," Margaret laughed. "He had always had a boat at home and enjoyed them very much. Instead of small boats, Bev was put on a horse. He patrolled the beaches on horseback, keeping watch for enemy ships and planes. Luckily, he was very familiar with horses. His family always had horses at their home near St. Michaels."

In 1944, Bev was transferred to Curtis Bay, near Baltimore, and he and Margaret once again began dating. On Valentine's Day 1945, the couple was married at Margaret's parents' home in Claiborne. "Because Bev was still in service, we lived in Baltimore,"

Margaret on the top step of the bank.
Courtesy of Margaret Sherman Bryan.

Margaret said. "We couldn't stand it! We were country people and the crowded conditions there bothered us, but we were very happy in spite of our living conditions. I worked as a secretary; Bev was an electrician's mate at the Coast Guard yard. He was discharged in 1946 and we continued to live in Baltimore for a while. Eventually, we returned to the Eastern Shore and bought a house in St. Michaels.

"Bev opened up a store in downtown St. Michaels where he did electrical repair and maintenance. I worked part-time in the local bank. The town was very safe. I could walk

Margaret and husband racing a Hampton sailboat.
Courtesy of Margaret Sherman Bryan.

down the street with $1,000 in cash to go from one bank to another and nobody would bother me. Eventually, I was employed full-time and worked my way up to head teller and, ultimately, to branch officer. I was in banking for over forty years before retirement in 1984. After retiring, I was appointed to the Advisory Board for a six-year term.

"Eventually, I gave birth to two boys. Chris is the oldest and Mark, the youngest. The Eastern Shore, Bev and I felt, was a much better environment for them than the city would have been."

Ever since he was a youngster growing up on the Eastern Shore, Bev had sailed on the tributaries of the Chesapeake Bay. Following their move back to St. Michaels, he built a Hampton sailboat that he named the *Leprechaun*. Bev built his boat in famed boat-builder Jim Richardson's yard, south of Cambridge. Richardson coached Bev as the boat neared completion.

The Hampton One Design sailboat was first built in 1934. Members of the Hampton (Va.) Yacht Club desired a sailboat that could be raced in shallow water. Over nine hundred of the sloops were eventually built. Carrying a two-person crew, the eighteen-foot boats were fast and responsive. On the East Coast, they became an active racing class.

"Bev loved sailing and I knew that I would be expected to join him on the water," said Margaret. "I learned to enjoy it, but preferred a relaxing style of sailing rather than racing. We had a total of three Hamptons altogether. Each of our Hamptons was named 'Leprechaun' and each was painted green. Hamptons are a very active racing class and Bev enjoyed racing in every part of the Bay. He was very competitive and usually was among the top three finishers in every race. I was his crew during the races. We competed for about ten years; eventually, our son, Chris, took over the crew responsibilities."

By 1952, over a million vehicles and two million passengers were crossing the Bay annually. In July of that year, the final ferry crossing was made from Annapolis to Matapeake. The massive Chesapeake Bay Bridge had been erected at a cost of $45 million and replaced the ferry system. The bridge spanned four and a half miles above the Chesapeake and was, at the time, the longest structure in the world over water. It was also the third longest bridge in the world at the time. Making a ceremonial final run, a ferry paralleled the bridge as cars whizzed by overhead. Aboard the ferry was the Governor of Maryland, Theodore McKeldin. B. Frank Sherman was at his side as it left Matapeake bound for Sandy Point.

Through the years, some notable individuals traveled on the ferries. In 1938, Ethel, Barbara, Margaret, and Frank were on one of the ferries traveling to Annapolis. "Daddy came up to the deck where we were sitting and told us to come and go with him," said Margaret. "We followed daddy to the stairway and he explained, 'I have someone I'd like you to meet.' We went down to the car deck and daddy walked over to one of the cars and President Franklin Delano Roosevelt was sitting inside. Daddy said, 'Mr. President,

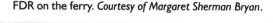

FDR on the ferry. *Courtesy of Margaret Sherman Bryan.*

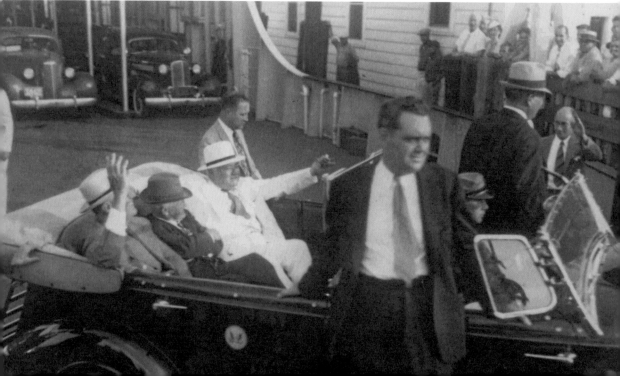

I'd like you to meet my daughters.' The President was quite jovial and Barbara and I were shocked and overjoyed, to say the least.

"The President had traveled from Washington on the Presidential Yacht *Potomac* and had delivered a speech in Denton. It was estimated that 9,000 people heard his speech from a podium set up across the street from the Caroline County Court House. He chose the ferry for his return trip to Washington."

The year 1938 was not the only time FDR made the trip from Washington to the Chesapeake. Three years earlier, he had traveled to the Eastern Shore in the presidential yacht, the *Potomac*, to take part in the opening of the Choptank River Bridge. On October 25, 1935, the bridge spanning the Choptank that linked the counties of Dorchester and Talbot opened. At the time, it was the longest bridge in the state. The *Potomac* was the first boat to go through the draw span of the bridge. Following dedication ceremonies, Roosevelt made a speech from the deck of the yacht. Coincidentally, seven-year-old Barbara Sherman, younger daughter of B. Frank Sherman, was one of three young ladies who cut the ribbon opening the bridge to traffic.

After the Bay Bridge opened, ferries continued making the Claiborne to Romancoke run until the end of the year. The final run was on December 31, 1952. Following the last run, B. Frank Sherman ended his 33-year career with the Chesapeake Bay Ferry System. During that time, an estimated twenty million passengers had used the ferry system.

"Daddy only enjoyed retirement for a short six years," stated Margaret. "In 1952, he and mother bought forty acres on Chance Point, near McDaniel, where they built a retirement home. In addition to the main house, there was a cottage on the property. Bev and I moved into the cottage and lived there until 1983. Located on the western side of Harris Creek, we had many good times traveling the rivers in our cabin cruiser. We had two of them. They were twenty-eight to thirty feet in length and we'd spend weekends and vacations on the boat. We'd often travel to Chestertown, Solomons, Cambridge,

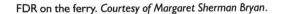

FDR on the ferry. *Courtesy of Margaret Sherman Bryan.*

B. Frank Sherman and Governor McKeldin.
Courtesy of Margaret Sherman Bryan.

and other places on the Western Shore. Bev, by then, was working at a marine supply business and knew lots of people at marinas all around the Bay. I really enjoyed our trips; it was relaxing to be out on the Bay or in a secluded anchorage.

"Mother died in 1983 and the place was sold. Bev and I bought a place nearby on Mallard Point. We had one and a half acres on the water there. In 1992, Bev passed away."

B. Frank Sherman was very active in civic endeavors. Twice he was Commodore of the Miles River Yacht Club in St. Michaels. He was founder and first President of the Chesapeake Bay Fishing Fair, as well as founder and initial President of the Talbot County Historical Society. He also founded and served as the first President of the Talbot County Chapter of the Isaac Walton League, a member of the Board of the St. Michaels Bank, and Chairman of the Board of Directors of an Annapolis bank.

"In the 1940s, there was a group that was advocating the building of an oil refinery in Talbot County near McDaniel," said Margaret. "The refinery was scheduled to be built on the shore of Eastern Bay. Daddy was vehemently opposed and led a group who successfully defeated the project.

"Daddy was quite a person. He loved the Eastern Shore and, particularly, Talbot County. He promoted the state and the Eastern Shore. Some people referred to him as the 'Ambassador of the Eastern Shore.' He was also called 'Mr. Eastern Shore.' He counted among his close friends top politicians at the state and national level. Numerous Governors were more than acquaintances. U.S. House Speaker Sam Rayburn was a close friend.

"He never met a stranger; he was friendly and knew everybody. He was a man of great integrity; he was honest and straight-forward. He had a certain charm that drew him close to all he met. In spite of the fact that he only had an eighth grade education, he was very successful as a businessman. He was self-educated and practical. Daddy was only sixty-six years old when he died in 1958. It seemed like a shame; he had so much more to give."

The opening of the Chesapeake Bay Bridge changed the Eastern Shore forever. No longer was the Bay the major highway over which passengers and goods were distributed. Spanning the width of the Bay was now a thin ribbon of steel that linked the two sides. Folks on the Eastern Shore were no longer isolated in remote villages.

In time, people from the more populated areas came to the Shore for relief from the pressures and tensions of urban life. Kent Island, at the foot of the bridge, was the first to experience widespread development. Settlers invaded the sleepy fishing community in droves and purchased lots the size of postage stamps. From their homes, it was an easy commute to jobs in Baltimore and Washington. The population swelled and, in time, the island more closely resembled Urbana than a laid-back fishing community.

Through the decades, the population migrated southward. Most of the towns on the Shore have felt the influx of the migration and the associated lifestyle changes. Except for geography, the Eastern Shore displays little resemblance to the place where B. Frank Sherman raised his family and became a legend.

To some, the changes that have occurred on the Shore are viewed with pessimism and negativity. These folks long for the days of yesteryear when men such as B. Frank Sherman were in their midst. Change, however, is inevitable. Perhaps the memory of men the caliber of Sherman will hasten their infusion into the place he held so dear.

Margaret Bryan enjoys reminiscing about the glory days when car-laden ferries crisscrossed the Chesapeake. Thoughts of her father are very much intertwined with those memories. She possesses many of the traits of her father. Kind, friendly, and compassionate, she is a fascinating lady. B. Frank Sherman would be most proud.

CHAPTER ELEVEN

Captain Linda Morgan

The northernmost river in the Bay is also the lengthiest in the entire watershed. The Susquehanna River meanders on a course of four hundred and forty-four miles from Cooperstown, New York, to its final destination, the Chesapeake. Twisting and turning around mountains, through rich farm lands, and major Pennsylvania cities, the river supplies the Chesapeake with half of its freshwater. At the end of its travels, where the river meets the Bay, lies the Harford County town of Havre de Grace.

Surrounded by a shallow bay called Susquehanna Flats, a century ago Havre de Grace was the upper Bay headquarters for duck hunters. The fertile waters of the Flats contained an endless supply of submerged grasses on which ducks fed. Hunters shot ducks by the hundreds; many for sport, others for profit. Havre de Grace became one of the most important towns in the northern Bay, with decoy production a major economic activity in the town. The town enjoyed a prosperity that many towns further south did not.

In time, the grasses once so prevalent began to die off and the complexion of the town changed. The town evolved into a center for boating activity, the role it currently enjoys. Accompanying the nautical atmosphere of the town was tourism. Townhouses and condos surrounded the multitude of marinas on the waterfront. In the neat downtown area, high-end restaurants and shops devoted to tourism proliferated. A pair of noteworthy museums came into being and a century-old lighthouse was restored and opened to the public. Tour boats docked near the center of town and tourists flocked to the area.

Captain Linda Morgan has lived in Havre de Grace for twenty years and sailed from there for forty. "I just love this area," she said. "This is truly home for me. Living any other place would be disappointing."

Linda operates the *Martha Lewis*, a skipjack that is owned by the Chesapeake Heritage Conservancy. Built in 1955 by famed boat-builder Bronza Parks in the southern Dorchester County town of Wingate, the *Martha* was one of three sister ships built

The MARTHA LEWIS. *Courtesy of Annie McLhinney-Cochran.*

simultaneously. For decades, the *Martha*, along with *Lady Katie* and *Rosa Parks*, enjoyed stellar careers dredging oysters on Chesapeake waters. Today, as the oyster population has waned and skipjack numbers have been drastically reduced, only a half-dozen skipjacks currently toil on oyster bars that were once so productive. A few of the historic vessels, like the *Martha Lewis*, have been preserved and are used for educational purposes.

"I thoroughly enjoy being the captain of the *Martha*," Linda Morgan explains. "There is nothing I enjoy more than having a group of school children out on the boat and watching the dredge come up filled with submerged aquatic vegetation. Once aboard, we identify the types of grasses and discuss how they are home to many species of Bay animals. I could do that everyday, year-round, and never tire of the job. I just love it."

In spite of the good times, Captain Linda found that skipjacks differed greatly from the traditionally-designed sailboats she was accustomed to operating. "It took me a while to learn the intricacies of a skipjack," she continued. "It took a couple of weeks to feel comfortable operating the boat; now I feel like it is an extension of my body."

Born in Elizabeth, New Jersey, Linda Morgan was introduced to sailing at an early age. "The best thing my parents ever did was move," the affable Morgan laughed. "We lived in Clinton, New Jersey, later moved to Syracuse, New York, and, in the mid-'60s, we relocated to Hockessin, Delaware. For me, that's where life began."

Linda's parents, Joe and Barbara Morgan, befriended a family named Diggs. "The Diggs family had a daughter and one day my dad and I joined them for a sail on their boat," she continued. "I remember that sail vividly. I was only seven or eight at the time. I really enjoyed being out there on the Bohemia River. I fell in love with sailing that day."

After chartering a few boats, the family purchased a Cal 25 they named *Persistence*. "I have a sister, Elaine, who is four years older," said Linda. "We cruised with the Columbia Sailing Association and began racing with them as well. I was the son my father never had and took to sailing with enthusiasm. Dad and I would hop in the car in the winter and drive down to the different points of land surrounding the top of the Bay. There, we'd study the way ice flows traveled around the points. That way we could better understand the way the current flows through the rivers."

Other boats followed the *Persistence*, each a bit larger and faster. Linda, however, during her high school years, began crewing on sailboats that raced out of Annapolis. "I crewed on a 36-footer named the *Havoc*," she said. "Crewing on that boat introduced me to another passion — delivering boats."

While crewing on the *Havoc*, Linda met Chuck Lilly. Chuck was very active in the yacht delivery business, and Linda crewed for him during boat deliveries for the next twenty years. "We delivered a boat named *Flaky Lady* from Rhode Island to the Chesapeake," she laughed. "I made enough money from that delivery to buy a car, a $400 Plymouth Valliant.

"My dad worked at Tidewater Marina in Havre de Grace. Tidewater sold new and used sailboats, in addition to operating a large marina. Often, when boats were purchased, the new owner wanted their boat delivered to other areas. Chuck and I would deliver those boats. We'd also bring boats back to Havre de Grace that had been traded in for new ones.

"Dad and I delivered sailboats to Florida twice in those years. We got on a Pearson with the owner and got as far as South Carolina and got hung up by a hurricane. The sailboat went on, but dad and I signed on to a fifty- or sixty-foot Burger, a fancy power yacht. It was owned by a hunchbacked Jewish man who was appalled that I couldn't operate anything in the galley. To him, the wheel house was no place for a female… that was my initial contact with discrimination. I was about twelve years old at the time."

Rather than attend college following graduation from high school in 1979, Linda delivered boats. Following her stint with Lilly, she has delivered yachts for the past ten years on her own. "This past October, I was delivering a 41-foot ketch from Cape Cod headed for North Carolina," Capt. Morgan said. "Tropical storm Sandy was bearing down and we'd gotten to New London, Connecticut. We weren't making good time. By then, we were aware that Sandy was now a full-blown hurricane and decided to remain in New London to ride out the storm. I identified a hurricane hole to wait out the storm and when I tried to start the engine to get the boat there, it wouldn't start. I tried everything I knew, but the engine failed to start. Finally, out of desperation, I dialed 1-800-Daddy-Help-Me-Please. Dad knows everything there is to know about marine engines. After getting him on the phone, he walked me through the problem and I was able to start the engine and motor over to the hurricane hole. We stripped the boat down, prepared her for the hurricane, rented a car, and came home."

For a long time, Linda delivered three or four boats every week. She estimates that she has delivered approximately 1,000 boats all over the East Coast during the past thirty years. Most of the deliveries have either began, or ended, in the Chesapeake Bay.

"I met a writer while delivering his boat from Annapolis to Long Island in 2010," Linda stated. "He is getting older, about seventy or so. He's a sailor who owns two boats. We've become good friends. I met him when I was hired to deliver his boat to Tidewater for winter storage. The following spring I was hired to return the boat to Kent Island. I called him to introduce myself because I felt he needed my services. He had many expensive upgrades done to the boat, but his dock lines were held together with duct tape. He didn't know how to tie a knot. We arranged to meet and now, fifteen years later, I still sail with him. Whenever he wants to go sailing, he calls me and I go with him. He wants me to take one of his boats to North Carolina and the other one to Florida. He keeps me pretty busy."

Often, Linda's daughter accompanies her on deliveries. Now twenty years old and a student specializing in environmental engineering at the University of Delaware, Elizabeth is a natural sailor. She and her mother lived on a 27-foot sailboat in Havre de Grace for eight years when she was much younger. "One day Elizabeth came home from school and said excitedly, 'Mommy, do you know that I'm the only kid in school that lives on a boat?'" Linda related. "She thought that all her classmates lived on boats.

"Elizabeth was on a delivery with me one time when she was nine years old. It was Mother's Day and she had explained that she wanted to navigate the boat from Havre de Grace to our destination, Rock Hall, all by herself. She wanted me to just chill out and relax. That was to be my Mother's Day present. It was a very hazy day; we were in a 45-foot sailboat. Elizabeth did a fantastic job. We had no problems getting to Rock Hall. She was amazing! We headed toward the dock and a group of men were standing around. They immediately began coaching her about how to get the boat into the slip. They're yelling at her, telling her how to do it, and she's telling them she can't hear them over the engine noise. I had trained her to only do what I suggested and not to listen to anyone else. She put the boat into the slip with no difficulty. After securing the boat, she shut down the engine, stood erect, looked at the group of men, and said, 'Now, what do you have to say about that?'"

Linda also has a 31-year-old son, Bobby, and he, too, is an accomplished sailor. He is the only person that Linda trusted to borrow her first sailboat. Currently, he does stage lighting for rock groups. "A couple of years ago he toured with the rock group Stone Temple Pilots for the summer," Linda said. "He's living the Rock & Roll dream. He also produces concerts on his own. Bobby and his friends produced a festive 'Ram Jam' involving art and music. The event was held in an outdoor venue and was very successful. He was an Eagle Scout. He trekked around Europe for several years; he inherited my love of traveling. He's a good kid."

For the past twenty-five years, Linda has held a U. S. Coast Guard license to operate boats for hire. During the past fifteen years, she has upgraded her license so she can captain boats with a gross weight up to one hundred tons. "I don't have any desire to operate a boat any larger than one hundred tons," she said. "I'm getting older and that's about the extent of what I want to do. I also have an old back injury that slows me down. I had a broken back in elementary school involving a seesaw. I didn't have it surgically repaired until 2011; it still gives me trouble from time to time."

Three months after her surgery, in a great deal of pain and nearly broke, Linda was asked to deliver a boat north. "I didn't want to do it, but I really needed the money," she said. "The boat was a 42-foot sailboat that drew seven feet of water. The owner had requested to come along and even brought along his crew. I don't usually want owners aboard when I make a delivery, but I was desperate. The owner was a Russian and he lived in Israel, where he had owned a large, very profitable business. Recently, he had sold the business to an American and he was in this country helping the new owner with the transition. He was the only person on board, other than me, who spoke English.

"My back was killing me. We sailed down Delaware Bay at night. The mast on the boat was so tall that we couldn't get under the bridge over the Cape May Canal. The only choice was to go around the Cape. On the ocean side, we headed into winds approaching forty knots and the water temperature was fifty-three degrees. The boat was low and flat, and spray was being thrown all over us. It was a new boat and there were no instruments on board, only a compass. There was not even a GPS or depth sounder. After a struggle, we sailed on to our destination. I returned home in terrific pain. After all that, the yacht broker who had arranged the delivery failed to pay me. Weeks later, after going back and forth, the boat manufacturer finally paid me. That was a miserable trip."

Linda was involved with the square rigged *Kalmar Nyckel* for fifteen years. The historical replica was built in Delaware and serves as a good will ambassador to ports all over the East Coast. "I was part of the builders' group," Linda explained. "I was a member of the first sail training crew. I was one of the people that would climb up into the tall rigging to furl and unfurl the square sails. I learned a lot from my experience with the *Kalmar Nyckel*. Eventually, though, I got too old to be climbing up those tall masts."

The master shipwright involved in building the *Kalmar Nyckel* also restored the *Martha Lewis* in 1995. He encouraged Linda to get involved with the volunteer crew of the skipjack. She agreed and was a crewmember for fifteen years prior to being appointed captain.

"During that time, I was working with a sailing school company called Baysail," Linda said. "I was one of the captains that would work with people, teaching them to sail. We had a classroom portion of the training and then we'd take them out on small sailboats to familiarize them with the fundamentals of sailing. Eventually, I was assigned to a cruising class. I'd take a group of people out on the Bay for a week at a time. We'd cruise to different ports on the Bay and I'd be teaching them sailing all the time. There was also a course that involved circumnavigating the entire Delmarva Peninsula. I circumnavigated Delmarva eleven times. We used boats over forty feet for this. It would take a week to travel the four hundred plus miles of the circumnavigation. The people were great to work with and it was an enjoyable experience.

"Boat owners found out about what I was doing with Baysail and would pay me to circumnavigate the Peninsula on their own boat. That was cool, but, eventually, I found myself waking up in the morning and wondering where I was. I guess it must be the same feeling that airline pilots get. I didn't like that feeling and wanted to do something else."

Linda decided to become involved in the health care field. "At first, I wanted to become a nurse, and then I thought, 'heck, might as well become a doctor,'" she stated. "I enrolled at the University of Maryland and I was two years into medical school. In September, I was supposed to report to the hospital in Havre de Grace to do an internship. I sat in my car outside the hospital and cried for three hours. I'd never worked inside a building before. The thought of going into a building and staying for the better part of a day was appalling to me. I changed my major to environmental science and dropped out of med school. I graduated in 2008.

"Until 2004, I'd never before been in debt. After college, I was severely in debt from student loans. I'm still trying to see my way clear of those obligations."

Captain Morgan worked for a short time running pilot boats out of Baltimore and Annapolis. Chesapeake Bay pilots are highly skilled captains who maneuver the deep drafted ships up and down the Chesapeake. Linda's job was to get the pilots out to assigned ships. "We'd take the pilots out to ships in a small boat," she said. "We'd travel out to a ship and pull alongside and wait while one pilot climbed up a rope ladder to get on the ship and the pilot being relieved climbed down to our boat before leaving and returning to the station.

"I did this job for six weeks, it was the worst job I've ever had. The pay was pitiful. Driving the boats was cool, but there was a lot of sitting around. One night, I was in the bathtub and the phone rang. I was requested to go to Baltimore for an assignment. When you got a call, you had to report in a matter of minutes to the station. I hurried and dressed, rushed out the door, and drove to Baltimore. In Baltimore, they put me

Captain Linda Morgan holding her citation.
Photo by author.

in a van and took me to Annapolis along with a pilot. I took him to a ship that was lying in the anchorage area, returned to Annapolis, and came home. After deducting my expenses, I calculated that I made $20 for that night of work. The company did offer good benefits, though. I blew out my knee and couldn't report for work for a while and lost that job just a few days short of being eligible for benefits."

For the last ten years, Linda has worked as a safety boat captain for Northeast Work and Safety Boats. Safety boats stand by as workers are engaged in activities involving bridge repair. The safety boat operator is needed in the event that a worker falls into the water.

"In December 2012, I reported for work," she said. "It was cold and miserable and I was really feeling bad from a virus. At the marina, where the safety boats are moored, there is a coffee shop. A lot of policemen hang out there before going to work. I go in there to fill up my thermos before getting on my boat. I told them as I was leaving, 'I sure hope nobody falls off that bridge today cause I feel lousy.' I got on my little safety boat named *Emily* and took my position under the Key Bridge in Baltimore. I wasn't there fifteen minutes when I looked up and saw a body free-falling through the air. I radioed in and said there was a body in the water and headed toward it. I could see debris on the water; a hat, shoes, etc. As I neared the spot, a head popped up. His eyes were open and they were vividly blue. I came alongside and threw him a life ring. I started talking and yelling at him; I could see that he was beginning to lose consciousness. By then, I had maneuvered *Emily* close to him. I ran out there and grabbed his shirt to keep his head above the water. People on the road deck above told me that 911 had been called. The man had attempted suicide. Water temperature was forty-eight degrees. A fishing boat came by and the owner pulled the man aboard. We cut off his clothes, wrapped him in dry clothing, and took him to shore. He had two broken legs and a broken back. We did all this in a span of fifteen minutes. An ambulance soon came and took him to the hospital.

"Engineers later calculated that when the man entered the water, he was traveling at fifty-seven miles per hour and submerged twenty-seven to thirty feet below the surface. The bridge deck was two hundred feet above the water.

"I really wanted to accompany him to the hospital because I felt a bond with him by that time. They didn't allow me to do that, but I knew where they had taken him and left a message for the family, saying I had hoped he would be okay. His mother called later, expressed her appreciation, and we now talk every month or so. I cried a lot after that experience. It was traumatic!" In March 2013, Linda was given a Life Saving Award by the transportation Authority Police for her unselfish acts at rescuing the man.

Captain Linda Morgan on the *Neptune's Pride*.
Courtesy of Annie McLhinney-Cochran.

Linda has worked at various bridges as captain of safety boats. In addition to the Key Bridge, she has worked under the Harry Nice Bridge over the Potomac River, the Susquehanna Bridge, Delaware River Bridge, Bear Creek Bridge, and the Chesapeake Bay Bridge.

"As a result of my running safety boats, I met my honey," she smiled. "I was told to report to the Bay Bridge and find an electrical worker named Charles Clouse. I found him, introduced myself, and told him I would be the captain of the safety boat and that I would be, 'At his service.' He did the Captain Morgan stance from the whiskey bottle and smiled at me. His company was rewiring the Bay Bridge. That day I met the love of my life two hundred feet above the waters of the Chesapeake Bay.

"I've done the marriage thing twice. I found that you can't turn a man into a sailor. I tried that two times and it never worked. I introduced Chuck to sailing and he loves it. He's a natural sailor and we bought a 33-foot boat (*Neptune's Pride*) together. I can't imagine life without owning a boat. We hope someday to sail into retirement. We hope to sail through the islands. My dream is to sail through the Panama Canal and visit the Galapagos Islands. Chuck thinks we should go to Florida and we may move the boat down there to be closer to the islands. There's really no place to sail in Florida unless you go offshore. I feel the Chesapeake is the best sailing spot in the entire U.S. Chuck is a great guy; we are committed to each other."

Now retired, Linda's parents live in Florida. "For a decade, after moving south, mom and dad lived on a sailboat," she explained. "At first, they lived on a 34-footer named the *Uncle Harry*. Uncle Harry was not really a family member, he was a good friend.

The *LANTERN QUEEN* tour boat. *Courtesy of Annie McLhinney-Cochran.*

When he died, he left them some money. They used their inheritance to buy the boat. Eventually, the 34-footer burned. The accident was due to faulty wiring from a toaster. They replaced it with a 42-footer they again named *Uncle Harry*. Aunt Ruth had been Uncle Harry's wife. They called the GPS on the boat Aunt Ruth because she was always telling Uncle Harry where to go. After mom retired, they spent winters in the Bahamas and summers on the Chesapeake. When mom got older, she suffered from a series of strokes and they sold the boat. I cried my eyes out when they sold that boat."

Linda's devotion to sailboats has enabled her to see a bit of the world outside the Chesapeake. "Boats got me to Israel," she said. "Mark Rosenburg was in a sailing class I taught at Baysail and he became interested in sailing. He went out with me on one of the week-long cruises and fell in love with sailing. I asked him where he was from and he said 'Jerusalem.' 'Is that in Pennsylvania?' I responded. 'No,' he said. 'The real Jerusalem?' One day I got a call from him asking me to come to Israel. He had bought a sailboat and wanted me to come over and teach him sailing. I ended up going over there three different times."

Boats also got Linda to Africa. "There was a 110-foot yacht originally built for the Canadian Navy just prior to World War II," Linda said. "The boat was never used during the war and ended up in the hands of Sam DuPont. DuPont had bought the boat from Ralph Evinrude (of the Evinrude outboard motor family) and his wife, actress Francis Langford. The name of the boat was *Enchantress* and it was moored on the Sassafras River. The owner of the *Lantern Queen*, a dinner cruise boat working out of Havre de Grace, bought it from DuPont. (I was the captain of the *Lantern Queen* for a while.)

"I ended up working on the *Enchantress* also. A guy named Joe Holt came to the boat to work on her. He was a great big guy, he was huge. He was very smart and worked on the systems that were on the boat. He and I got to be good friends. Joe had been an airplane expert before starting Holt Marine Systems. He was highly skilled. We maintained contact for some time. Eventually, he went back to working on airplanes.

"The day before I was to take a final exam at College Park, Joe sent me an e-mail inviting me to come to Africa. I finished my exam the next day and, as I was handing it to my instructor, I told him, 'I'm going to Nairobi.' A couple of days later, I was on a plane headed to Africa. Joe and I were all over Africa working on airplanes. I was chased by baboons in a national park. I got out of Joe's vehicle to go to the bathroom and a baboon started chasing me. I looked down and there were five, then ten. The attendant opened the door for me and was bent over double laughing. Baboons are ugly; the closer you get to them the uglier they get. The trip was eventful."

Captain Morgan at the helm of the *Martha Lewis*. Photo courtesy of Annie McLhinney-Cochran.

Linda was also involved with the National Oceanic and Atmospheric Association (NOAA). At first, she was a volunteer and later a paid employee. Working out of Woods Hole, Massachusetts, she was assigned to the research vessel *Albatross*. "I was one of the scientists on board," she said. "We were on the boat for six months at a time and cruised from Iceland to Hatteras. We would tow a trawl net, then examine the variety of species we caught for the purpose of deciding the health of the fishery. It was very interesting. Had I not met Chuck, I might have stayed on and made it a career."

Linda feels that every experience has prepared her for her role on the *Martha Lewis*. "All my experiences have groomed me for working on that boat," she said. "Working on the *Martha* is all I really ever want to do. It seems like I'm destined to work on that boat."

Sadly, however, Linda learned that the *Martha Lewis* will probably not be sailing during the 2013 season. "I was just told that she needs a new mast," she explained. "A new mast will cost between $20,000 and $40,000. It is very unlikely that we'll be able to raise that kind of money in time for the sailing season, so, at least for now, I'm out of a summer job. It is devastating."

Linda is also concerned about the health of the Chesapeake. "A couple of years ago tropical storm Lee swept through the area," she said. "The storm brought with it an incredible amount of rain that washed lots of silt, previously trapped behind the Conowingo Dam, into the Susquehanna. There was so much silt that it traveled all the way down the Bay to Tilghman Island. The silt smothered all the oysters above the Bay

Sunset over Havre de Grace marina.
Courtesy of Annie McLhinney-Cochran.

Bridge. The Dam is a big problem because of the silt that is trapped behind it. The water quality in Havre de Grace is so bad that most people won't think of swimming in it. If you do swim in the Susquehanna, you're likely to get an ear infection or worse.

"Because of the silt washing down, the water depth in Havre de Grace has been reduced drastically. Where the water depth was once fifteen feet in one marina, it is now less than six feet. I'm concerned now that I won't have a place to keep my boat. On low tide, I can't get my sailboat out of the slip she is in because of the lack of water depth."

In spite of all the negatives, Linda remains strongly attached to the Chesapeake Bay. "The Bay is the greatest sailing area anywhere," she said. "It is comfortable and incredibly safe because it is confined and protected. The Bay offers so much diversity. On the Eastern Shore, there are lots of creeks to duck into and explore a great place to go gunkholing. The other shore is less isolated and more urban. There are lots of neat people in the area from differing walks of life. The diversity of the area makes it very appealing.

"My life started on the Chesapeake Bay. It is comfortable, it is my home. I can't think of any place I'd rather be. It's a beautiful part of the world."

Afterword

Like the characters in an earlier work (*Chesapeake Men*), the women discussed in the preceding pages were greatly influenced by the Chesapeake Bay. For some, this resulted in career choices that necessitated direct interaction with the Bay on a daily basis. For others, the magnificent Chesapeake provided the inspiration and motivation for their life's work. All, however, have a deep respect for the Bay, its beauty, and its magnetism.

Not appreciably different, in many ways, from their counterparts in *Chesapeake Men*, these women are strong of character and steadfast in their beliefs. They are honest and sincere, strong-willed, and intense. They reflect wholesome values instilled by previous generations, and possess an inner satisfaction from a lifetime of good deeds and positive interaction with their fellow human beings.

These ladies are appreciative of the Chesapeake culture and heritage in which they interact. Even those that came from distant environments are in awe of the shadows cast by the Bay. They have adapted to the Eastern Shore way of life and made it their own.

It has been truly a pleasure to have interacted with the men and women in the compilation of both books, *Chesapeake Men* and *Chesapeake Women*. Their stories and memories have been delightful. Interacting with them has been extremely gratifying. Hopefully the friendships that resulted will endure for many years to come.